P9-EEQ-958

*Writing Tom Sawyer*

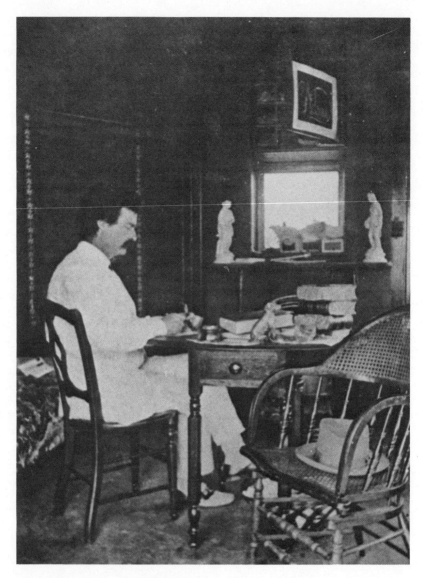

*Mark Twain at work in his Quarry Farm study; about 1876 or shortly thereafter. The small bright window over the fireplace was bricked in not long after.*

# Writing Tom Sawyer

## The Adventures
## of a Classic

*by Charles A. Norton*

*McFarland & Company, Inc., Publishers*
*Jefferson, North Carolina, and London*
1983

For permission to include in this volume certain illustrative materials, quotations, and previously unpublished material, or for assistance in obtaining material, the following are acknowledged: *Frontispiece* (photo of Twain in his Quarry Farm study) Chemung County Historical Society, Elmira, N.Y.; *photographs on pages 5 and 28* (pages of the original manuscript) Georgetown University Library Special Collections Division, Washington, D.C.; *passim* (material reprinted from books by Twain) Harper & Row, Publishers, Inc. New York; *page 50 top left* (photo of Laura Hawkins) Mark Twain Papers, Bancroft Library, University of California, Berkeley; *page 50 top right* (photo of Olivia Langdon) Jervis Langdon, Quarry Farm, Elmira, N.Y.; *page 50 bottom right* (photo of Jane Clemens) Ralph Connor, Fort Lauderdale, Fla.; quotation from *The Curious Death of the Novel*, Louisiana State University Press, Baton Rouge. For aid in preparation of Appendix II, thanks go to Mildred Abraham, University of Virginia, Charlottesville.

**Library of Congress Cataloging in Publication Data**

Norton, Charles A.
  *Writing Tom Sawyer.*

  Bibliography: p.
  Includes index.
  1. Twain, Mark, 1835–1910. Adventures of Tom
Sawyer. I. Title.
PS1306.N67 1982    813'.4    82-17164

ISBN 0-89950-067-6

Manufactured in the United States of America

# Acknowledgments

Ten years have gone into the research and writing of this book. Frequently, those approached by the author for aid were cooperative beyond expectations. When publication seemed far off, and sometimes unlikely, there were always some persons present to issue encouraging words.

Because of the length of time required for the research and writing, the miles covered literally, visiting the locales important to Mark Twain and *The Adventures of Tom Sawyer*, conferring with and listening to many individuals in the process, it is unlikely that a complete accounting could be made of everyone who contributed to the author's efforts. For these reasons, many must be thanked en masse.

There are some acknowledgments, however, that deserve special attention. The aid provided by the Miami University Library, Oxford, Ohio, both by the staff when I worked there as a staff member and later as I returned to do research, stands foremost. A special thanks to Edgar M. Branch, among our outstanding Mark Twain scholars, whose research office is located in the Miami University King Library, for offering incentive and encouragements from time to time. Thanks also to Walter Havighurst for encouraging words. My gratitude to all of the others connected with the Miami University Library.

For access to the *Tom Sawyer* manuscripts and other valuable aid, I owe special thanks to Ralph Gregory, formerly curator of the Mark Twain Memorial Shrine in Florida, Missouri, and to George M. Barringer, special collections librarian at the Georgetown University Library, Washington, D.C.

Acknowledgment must be made for the aid furnished by various organizations featuring or including valuable Mark Twain research materials: the Mark Twain Research Foundation, the Missouri University Library, the Mark Twain Museum, the Mark Twain Memorial, the Mark Twain Society, Elmira College, the Mark Twain Papers, and others.

Thanks also to Harper & Row, Publishers, Inc. for allowing the inclusion of material reprinted from Mark Twain's writings; from *Mark Twain: A Biography* by A.B. Paine; and from *Mark Twain in Eruption*, edited by Bernard DeVoto. Thanks to Louisiana State University Press for use of a quotation from *The Curious Death of the Novel: Essays in American Literature* by Louis D. Rubin, Jr.

Many books and articles, most noted in the text but too many to repeat here, without which this book could not have been completed, deserve more recognition that I can properly provide. Over a dozen checklists and bibliographies, perhaps the most notable of which was

*Mark Twain: A Reference Guide*, compiled by Thomas Asa Tenny and published by G.K. Hall, made substantial contributions to the book.

Finally, thanks go to a number of supportive friends my experience as a writer brought me into association with, and to the members of my family, especially Harriet, my wife, for her aid and support for all of these years.

Keeping in mind especially the future readers of Mark Twain who may find this book valuable, I want to dedicate it to my grandchildren with deepest love and affection.

# Table of Contents

# Preface

Recognition of Mark Twain's *The Adventures of Tom Sawyer* as an established classic for children is nearly universal. Many recall it as an innocent tale. They recall its childhood adventures as forming a narrative of a mid-nineteenth century summer. Accordingly, they usually rate it an easy and always entertaining story for children to read.

It is all of this. Its far-reaching reputation as a recommendable book for juvenile readers is fully legitimate.

This opinion, however, overlooks the fact that Mark Twain began to write *Tom Sawyer* as a novel for adult readers and even defended it as such at times.

This status of *Tom Sawyer* as a popular classic for children therefore requires special efforts to convince readers it is actually something more. A number of scholars and critics fortunately have seen greater value in this novel. It is gradually earning an improved reputation. Close readings have resulted in the growing recognition that it is beyond just a "hymn to boyhood." Many of these scholars and critics have managed to discover profound themes running through the pages of *Tom Sawyer*, though the critical attention it receives is nowhere equal to that given its sequel, *The Adventures of Huckleberry Finn*, nor can it ever expect the same.

It has never lacked readers, yet many may not realize that, apparently with some conscious intentions, Mark Twain planned it as a more complex novel. It does more than merely recall the years of a Middle American childhood.

This novel deserves a more prominent place among the writings of Mark Twain and in American literature; it has an importance to his career never properly given its due. It was created at the peak of his power as a writer.

If *Tom Sawyer* is more than a straightforward novel for children, certain questions arise. Why did Mark Twain write it? When did he work on the writing of it? What are the real values of its story?

# Part I

## *Creating the Story*

# 1. An Aborted Beginning (1872–January 1873)

Writing *The Adventures of Tom Sawyer* became a new and extended series of adventures for Mark Twain. It was the result of his first serious attempt to create a long work of fiction. Before beginning work on this novel, the author's experience with fiction writing was on a secondary level. He was an accomplished journalist — the author of numerous sketches with two subscription-sold books based on series of these sketches, and a popular lecturer noted for his humor and his delivery of it — but not a novelist.

Twain was not a stranger to the mechanics of fiction when he began to work on *Tom Sawyer*. Much of his previous work used similar techniques. Dialogue and characterization were already common in his writings, beginning as early as his Hannibal days. Fiction was a major item among the ingredients he used to construct his sketches and his lecture materials. There were occasions when he even made use of pure fiction in some of his work, but for a large part it was a minor use of fiction hung on a factual framework devised from personal experiences.

He began writing about the adventures of Tom Sawyer in 1872, although the basic idea had been developing over a number of years. In fact he had made a less successful start in 1870 on material that was to form the basis for the opening of *Tom Sawyer*, a time shortly after his marriage to Olivia Langdon in Elmira, N.Y. He laid that initial effort aside soon after he began it and engaged himself in work he was more accomplished at and saw as more profitable, writing the semiautobiographical *Roughing It*.

The desire to write fiction was a strong force. Mark Twain, first of all, was a story teller. He had begun learning that art early and pursued it all through his apprentice years. Exaggeration vied with truth in the material he wrote as a journalist. His ability as a story teller made him a successful lecturer wherever he went. It was, perhaps, in preparing lecture materials that the author invented Tom Sawyer as a character, basically formed as a fictional character, but one on which he could impose some of the autobiographical materials he usually worked with.

There is a frustrating lack of hard evidence as to when and where Twain actually began writing the material that would eventually become the novel. There are disconnected facts and gaps in the information that leave no recourse but speculation for some of the work's history. The few serious attempts to treat the work's development have always used knowledgeable guesses in the assignment of some dates and places.

Whether consciously or inadvertently, Twain vouchsafed to us only a smattering of vital information regarding the writing of *Tom Sawyer*. The sources are various. Much of the best of the information comes from his letters, particularly a few exchanged with William Dean Howells, these useful mostly in treating the final months of efforts to arrange the manuscript for publication. Other information can be uncovered in the manuscripts, the original and the copy manuscript, although they are subject to varying interpretations. Some of the biographical material, particularly that in the famed biography of the author by Albert Bigelow Paine, is helpful. Paine's work is important because of the personal contact with the author in the last years. Also useful, but again subject to varying interpretations because they are not always complete and accurate, are a number of reminiscences and recollections supplied by the author.

One recollection produced with the intention that it be used for his *Autobiography*, but only published later as a part of *Mark Twain in Eruption*, a collection of various autobiographical items edited by Bernard DeVoto, furnishes positive evidence for assuming the 1872 date. In a dictation during the summer of 1907, Twain related the following:

> The Garrick was familiar to me; I had often fed there in bygone years as a guest of Henry Irving ... and other actors.... It could have been there, but I think it was at Bateman's, thirty-five years ago, that I told Irving and Wills, the playwright, about the whitewashing of the fence by Tom Sawyer, and thereby captured a chapter on cheap terms; for I wrote it out when I got back to the hotel while it was fresh in mind.

The author's belief this had happened "thirty-five years ago" would place the event in 1872. The reliability of this reminiscence is an open question, considering that not all of the author's autobiographical materials are always accurate, being faulty because of either the failures of memory, the needs of the creative process, or the intent of their author. Some doubt has been cast upon this recollection of the meeting with Sir Henry Irving because there is no other mention of Irving in the records of Twain prior to a letter written in 1873 when the author was on his second trip to England.

It was in 1872 that he made his first visit there. In many ways it was a triumphant trip, for Mark Twain was already beginning to be known and read in England. He sailed for England late in August and did not return home until the end of November. Aggressively pursuing the beginnings of fame, he met with many influential and talented people during the months he spent in England, attending dinners at various clubs and elsewhere at a steady pace. Since the recollection notes that he "often" dined with Irving, a reference to later as well as earlier meetings, and since Irving was in London in the fall of 1872 and likely at some of the same dinner parties that Twain attended, possibilities that the two men met a year before Irving was mentioned in any letter remain reasonable.

Evidence much firmer, however, exists that Mark Twain was in the process late in 1872 of writing some of the manuscript pages which form the opening chapters of *Tom Sawyer*. There is definitive evidence given in the first 118 pages of the original manuscript that realistically confirms these pages were done in the period immediately prior to January 1873. This evidence comes from a comparison of the paper used for the manuscript along with an equating of the style of the writing on those pages using examples that can be stated as belonging to this period. While it can be speculated that he wrote more than these 118 pages, they are definitely singled out easily because following these the size of the paper changes, as does the style of the penmanship, indicating that the later pages of the manuscript at this point were done in greater haste.

This is not the only convincing proof of the existence of the first part of the *Tom Sawyer* manuscript for this period. What seems indisputable evidence is found as a part of a note the author placed in a corner of page 23 of his original manuscript. This page, incidentally, is the opening page of Chapter II, the chapter in which "the whitewashing of the fence by Tom Sawyer" is narrated, the same chapter the author declared he had written after his meeting with Irving while on a visit to England. The note reads:

> Never forget the splendid jewelry that illuminated the trees on the morning of Jan. 9, '73. Brilliant sun & gentle, swaying wind — deep, crusted snow on ground — all the forest gorgeous with gems — yellow & white diamonds, rubies, emeralds, fine opals, all with an inconceivably blinding flash to them when you were *between* them & the sun — but looking *toward* the sun, the trees (close at hand or overhead) were beads & wires of crystal — further away they were intricately meshed & webbed with shining gossamer threads — in the distance the forest seemed vague & pallid — something as if a powdery snowfall were intervening.

The author thoughtfully added "(descending among the branches)" following "intervening." Elsewhere on the page, he noted: "No overcoat needed, even when standing still." If any other proof of the authenticity of the date is needed it is found in the immediacy of the note's language.

Bernard DeVoto, the first, apparently, to make public notice of this note, objected to acceptance of the note as having been made on the date which it incorporates. First in the Limited Editions Club's *Tom Sawyer* and later as a part of his book *Mark Twain at Work*, while DeVoto seems willing to concede, regarding the history of Twain's note, that "He was certainly working on *Tom Sawyer* when he made the note," he qualifies this by brashly adding, "but he did not necessarily make it on the date it refers to." Such an argument seems to serve no purpose other than to defend the general belief that *Tom Sawyer* was written solely in 1874 and 1875.

DeVoto was correct in asserting that the ice storm the note refers to had made quite a strong impression on Twain. Years later in *Following*

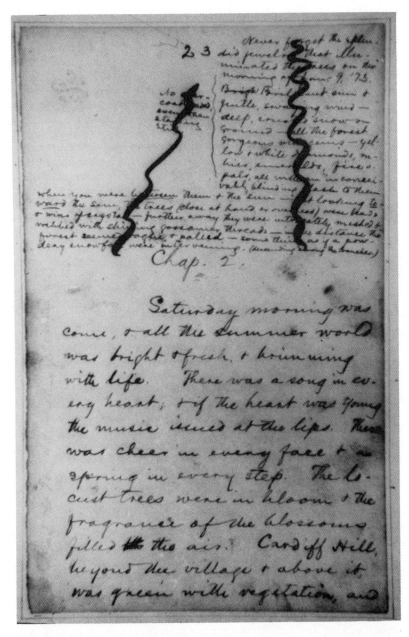

*Page 23 of the original manuscript for* The Adventures of Tom Sawyer, *the beginning of Chapter II, bears the ice storm note dated "Jan. 9, '73" indicating this page of the manuscript was in existence at this time or earlier. Courtesy of the Georgetown University Library.*

*the Equator*, written for the most part in 1896, the author describes a similar ice storm. However by then he could have witnessed many other similar storms. DeVoto's argument has no firm basis and the date which the note contains can be accepted as establishing the date when it was recorded.

Other proof of its authenticity and of the existence therefore of at least this part of the *Tom Sawyer* manuscript can be deduced from the fact that Twain's wife wrote a letter to her mother at this same time in which she describes the same ice storm. The question of why the author made the note where he wrote it is open to speculation. It can be visualized that he was continuing to struggle with the opening chapters of his manuscript at this time, and upon seeing the enchanting wintery scene he recorded it as a note for later incorporation in the novel, as he did with various other items. This can explain the note, for although *Tom Sawyer* as published uses only the days of an extended summer for its time frame, at this point Twain still entertained plans for the writing of a much longer novel more appropriate for publication as a subscription book offering. Later, when he had no longer a need for the note, he crossed it out.

It can be seen that the author had by the first days of 1873 made a start on his *Tom Sawyer* manuscript. It is fair, if only speculative, to see him as having already spent many hours of many days over the several preceding months wrestling with it. When inspired, the writing came easily and he spent long stretches accumulating manuscript pages. At other times as the material for the story eluded him, he discovered himself struggling word by word, or not writing at all. At this stage he frequently discarded or set aside material equal in quantity to that which he kept for his intended manuscript.

While only these 118 pages may confidently be indicated as work of this period which was retained for use in the final manuscript, these pages lead to the suggestion that there was more earlier and that this is only a remnant of work completed earlier. The evidence is not concrete, but there are a number of reasons, including some found in the author's recollections, to believe that the author had probably written, by the end of the first phase of the writing of *Tom Sawyer*, in early January 1873, a manuscript totaling some 400 pages. In more than one instance there is evidence given or stated that it was typical for Twain to produce about 400 pages of manuscript during periods when he was inspired and working hard on a project. At such times he wrote steadily, writing and rewriting, keeping pages and throwing discarded pages into a convenient fire.

A strong indication of there having earlier been a manuscript of more than 118 pages at this time is the manner in which the first eight chapters of *Tom Sawyer* follow a similar pattern, also short parts of later chapters. These differ sharply from the remaining parts of the book. What mainly sets these first eight chapters off is their obvious sketch-like quality. They aim sharply at describing Tom Sawyer as a "bad boy" as he experiences a number of events bearing little relation to the later adventures. In both their style and content they are more sketches than chapters of a novel with a plot. The references in these to the plot, being few in number, were most likely included at a later period, becoming a part of these pages in 1874. If the theory is correct that approximately 400 pages had resulted from this first phase, then these consisted of the 118 pages which still exist, incorporated into the manuscript with only minor revisions; another approximately 107 pages wholly rewritten to form the remaining pages necessary for the first eight chapters of the book; and some 175 pages, more or less, from which he adapted portions for later chapters, or otherwise discarded when work on the manuscript was renewed after a lapse of some 14 months while the manuscript went untouched.

This "lapse" helps to confirm this appraisal through another reminiscence referring to work done on Tom Sawyer. This recollection is again found as a part of *Mark Twain in Eruption*:

> It was by accident that I found out that a book is pretty sure to get tired, along about the middle, and refuse to go on with its work until its powers and its interest should have been refreshed by lapse of time. It was when I had reached the middle of *Tom Sawyer* that I made this invaluable find. At page 400 of my manuscript the story made a sudden and determined halt and refused to proceed another step. Day after day it still refused. I was disappointed, distressed and immeasurably astonished, for I knew quite well that the tale was not finished and I could not understand why I was not able to go on with it. The reason was very simple — my tank had run dry; it was empty; the stock of materials in it was exhausted; the story could not go on without materials; it could not be wrought out of nothing.
>
> When the manuscript had laid in a pigeonhole two years I took it out one day and read the last chapter that I had written. It was then that I made the great discovery that when the tank runs dry you've only to leave it alone and it will fill up again in time, while you are asleep — also while you are at work at other things and are quite unaware that this unconscious and profitable cerebration is going on. There was plenty of material now, and the book went on and finished itself without any trouble.

What seems to have occurred is described here with varying degrees of accuracy, some parts being misleading if not inaccurate assertions, and other parts needing to be judged carefully in order to be correctly interpreted.

Does this statement, which bears no date, refer to the writing done initially in the winter of 1872–1873 and to the suspected 400 pages of manuscript that may have been produced? If this is a correct assessment of the recollection, it then explains, if only abstractly, why the manuscript was laid aside in January of 1873 and work not resumed upon it until "two years" later in mid-spring of 1874.

Some people attempting to chronicle the writing of *Tom Sawyer* have assumed that the halt in the writing took place at the end of the summer of 1874, with the effort being resumed in June of 1875. This seems unlikely as it requires the lapse of "two years" to be a mere nine months, an unneccesary distortion of the recollection. If it is assumed, however, that the times of the events here referred to be late 1872 for the halt occurring and mid-spring of 1874 for a resumption of the work, then the lapse becomes about fourteen months. What seems likely is that when the recollection was composed, the author mentally subtracted the one year from the other and came up with "two years" as a convenience to recalling the number of months. Adding to the belief that this refers to the earlier dates is the fact that it can be successfully argued that Mark Twain had neither the inspiration nor the time he needed in 1875 to complete the last half of *Tom Sawyer*, a portion notable for its superior content.

What seems to have happened, and is described here, is that the work on the *Tom Sawyer* manuscript had grown "tired" later in 1872, for even considering that the author was familiar with many of the techniques of fiction, he was not accustomed to the plotting of a novel. Having reached a point some "400" pages into the effort, "the story made a sudden and determined halt and refused to proceed another step." It possibly refused because, after struggling with the material over a period of weeks, it remained more a collection of sketches rather than a plotted novel. As the author realized this, because he had nothing with which to build upon for the remaining pages of the novel, he became "disappointed" and "distressed." As he noted, "Day after day it still refused." Each day that the work was delayed, enthusiasm for it dwindled.

At this point, he turned to the nearest help, his next-door neighbor, Charles Dudley Warner. While not a novelist, but a journalist and an author of sketches, as was Twain, Warner was willing to discuss the plotting problems of his author neighbor. The two men often conversed as they walked home from church, or during one of the regular visits exchanged between the two houses. Twain hoped that such a discussion would aid him in finding a means of adding a usable plot to his novel, thus allowing him to resume work on it. This did not happen—but during these talks, some of which were directed at the plotting of current novels for that period, came a decision to attempt to coauthor a novel.

> The idea appealed to Warner, and there was no delay in beginning. Clemens immediately set to work and completed 399 pages of manuscript, the first eleven chapters of the book, before the early flush of enthusiasm waned.

In this way is the start, in mid-January 1873, of the work on the novel *The Gilded Age* described by Mark Twain's biographer, Albert Bigelow Paine.

Perhaps the rapid start on the jointly authored novel was the result of Twain's having mulled over various materials for possible use in *Tom Sawyer* that he chose not to retain for that work. Whatever the reason, this material, which is also based generally on bits about the author's family's coming to Missouri and later events, was offered as the start for *The Gilded Age*. These parts are not concerned with the Hannibal experiences, which had a special sentimental attachment for the author, an unspoken value then and later, so he was both able and pleased to put them to a profitable use. With this start on the novel, that is often mistakenly regarded as Twain's initial attempt at the writing of fiction, the author stored *Tom Sawyer*'s pages in the "pigeonhole" of his desk until his "tank" should "fill up again in time."

The coauthored novel completed that spring, Mark Twain took his family to England for a long "holiday." Late in 1873 he returned his young daughter and pregnant wife, only to resail to England to complete a series of lectures. There is little to indicate any activity toward serious, inspired writing during this interlude. He was contented with the many accolades heaped upon him by his British friends.

Meanwhile, as he later recalled, the chance for "unconscious and profitable cerebration" was happening to him. Almost without exception Twain appeared to need a moving inspiration in order to begin working steadily on a project. With *Tom Sawyer* set aside, not knowing whether he would take it up again or go on to some other work, he awaited for such inspiration to strike anew. He did not need to wait too long. The required inspiration appeared in 1874, suddenly and conveniently triggered by a newspaper article that he was certain to have read.

# 2. The "Tank" Is Refilled
# (1874)

That a newspaper article furnished an idea for the plot in Mark Twain's *Tom Sawyer* is not unlikely. Such a source had furnished suggestions for parts of the plot material used in *The Gilded Age*. Although there is no confirming statement from the author, and though the plot needed to be elaborated upon through many pages of writing, the key element was probably discovered in a news item.

There are several ways in which this article could have come to Twain's attention at this time. It is obvious that newspapers were the leading source of information for most people during the later years of the 19th century. Those wanting to keep in touch with events happening in their world subscribed to at least one paper and often to several, as Twain did. His extensive and personal association with the writing and printing of the news made such publications even more important to him than to most persons. He had a dependency on them. They were a daily habit, the main window through which to observe the world at large. Also, with many people at that time, it was a common practice to include clippings of interest when mailing letters to family members. The members of Twain's family, especially his mother and his brother, made a regular habit of sending clippings of items that they suspected would have interest for their son and brother. While Mark Twain probably subscribed to and read many papers, his birth in Missouri and his early years there would have led him to read regularly such a paper as the St. Louis *Democrat* as a source of news from "home."

Whatever the means that it reached him, when the *Democrat* published on April 7, 1874, a prominent article dealing with "Mc-Dowell's" cave in Hannibal, Mark Twain had sufficient opportunities to see the item. "THE CAVE AT HANNIBAL (A LETTER TO THE EDITOR)" was announced in an upper-case headline at the top of page 2 where it would have quickly caught the attention of any native of Hannibal. That this cave had a prominent place in his mind is shown in his first important book, written just a couple of years before his work on *Tom Sawyer*. There, he explains:

> the memory of a cave I used to know at home was always in my mind, with its lofty passages, its silence and solitude, its shrouding gloom, its sepulchral echoes, its flitting lights, and more than all, its sudden revelations of branching crevices and corridors where we least expected them.

The writer of the letter published in the St. Louis *Democrat*, impressed much as Twain had been, noted that the Hannibal cave was a "wonderful formation." After giving a description of its location, the correspondent told of having visited the place with a small group of individuals, including a guide and other members of the press, each given a torch to carry. Most of the main features or formations are then noted by their names and described in some detail. The writer reported seeing bats by the thousands, and spoke of "galleries in ever direction." Evidence was viewed that Abraham Lincoln had visited the cave in 1834. His name, among many others, had been inscribed on the walls of the cave. The writer of the article also comments that Twain had been in the cave, saying "By the way, Mr. Clemens used to reside in Hannibal." (This, surely, if there was no other reason, would have insured that such an item would find its way to Twain.) The tour, according to the correspondent, ended with the guide's pointing out passages that ran to "depths unknown." However, the most significant statement of the article comes near its conclusion, where the unknown writer calculates:

> A thousand weird tales are told about the cave. It is strange that some enterprising story-teller has not seized up it as the locality of some blood and thunder novel.

Twain must have taken that fortunate statement to be an invitation to plot a story around some boyhood knowledge he remembered about the cave. The date of this article's appearance is important as it came at a time when Mark Twain and his family were preparing to make a journey from their Hartford residence to Elmira, N.Y., and up to Quarry Farm for the months of the summer. It was a critical time for the author, for it can be seen now that he was at the outset of one of the strongest creative periods of his career. There is a good chance that he saw the article about the cave just about the time he was trying to decide what work he should take along with him to occupy his attention during the next several months.

The importance of working on another book was foremost in his plans. It had been a year since he had completed the novel with Warner as the coauthor. He was determined to become a man of letters, earning his income principally from books, giving up lecturing because of the long absences from his family along with the many wearying discomforts of constant travel. Upon reading the suggestion that "some enterprising story-teller" should use the cave as a setting for a "blood and thunder novel," Twain recognized it as an opportunity to salvage a part of the approximate 400 pages of manuscript he had stored away. He must have immediately seen that here was a place in which he could use the childhood incidents, then consisting mostly of pages of humorous sketsketches, involving Tom Sawyer. Taking out the manuscript pages he had preserved from late 1872 and early 1873, he reread them to see how a plot might now be fitted around them, consisting of an adventure story, and aimed at making some use of the cave.

Those pages had probably not been touched since the author had undertaken the task of writing *The Gilded Age* with Warner. In his thoughts regarding a theme for that novel, he had for a part of the time seen it as a satire reflecting upon the manners of the popular romantic novel. Now, the author thought that he might follow that notion in a similar way by attempting a satire on the blood and thunder novel. It was typical of his thinking that this would have appealed to him more than the idea of writing a straight adventure type novel. He had a commanding desire to reach the largest possible audience. These he wanted to disturb with his fervent morality—but under the disguise of humor. It was this type of writing which best fired the furnace of his imagination. How soon, and how easily, the basic plot that is found in the novel took shape after he picked up the earlier written pages and reread them is not known. An examination of the original manuscript suggests that this plot developed in uncertain steps. He probably had learned some lessons from his work on the novel written with Warner—that he must allow certain elements of the manuscript already written to direct the plot of the succeeding portions of the work. Still, narrating a plot to fit the unrelated incidents in this case did not come any easier than plotting normally did for Mark Twain. There are signs that he struggled with the difficulties and problems of creating a suitable plot. He, like many authors who depend heavily upon the resources of inspiration, could create brilliant vignettes with ease—however, many critics agree on the fact that because of this dependency almost all of his longer narratives, even the finest, are flawed with stretches of unsatisfactory work.

Having made a fresh start on his manuscript with the intention of building a plot about the cave to put new material into his Tom Sawyer sketches, following his reading of the article in April of 1874, he packed the manuscript in his bags as the family prepared to go to Elmira for several months. One of the principle reasons for going there was that his wife wanted to be near her mother for the birth of their next child. By the time the family had arrived in May at Quarry Farm, the home of his wife's sister, he had already developed some definite ideas for adding the additional chapters that would turn his Tom Sawyer sketches into an exciting "blood and thunder" novel. From the pirate games that Tom and his friends engaged in, he developed the idea of introducing actual pirates, similar to those who had been associated with John Murrell, a fabled criminal roaming the Mississippi basin during the author's boyhood. From the idea of the pirates he developed the idea of introducing an actual treasury cache. At the core of his idea for real pirates he saw that he needed to develop a villain. One of his original thoughts considered using the drunken father of Huckleberry Finn as a member of the criminal band, as can be seen from changes in the original manuscript. Also, he toyed at one time with some thoughts as to using a character who would represent the acceptable, good society, patterned after his beloved uncle, John Quarles, a man he idolized more than his own father.

Somewhere, along the way, as the plot began to develop in his imagination, working step by step, he finally decided upon using as his chief villain a half-breed Indian. Such characters were frequently to be found in the territory of Twain's youth. Such individuals were normally considered outcasts and were frequently referred to for frightening small children. In this way, they often became a vague part of the myths developed in groups of boys who were growing up in Twain's day. From a literary point of view, the romantic Indian fallen in grace because of the strains of civilization provided an ideal character, one full of attractive possibilities. Whether Mark Twain patterned this character, Injun Joe, on one he had known in his youth, or not, has never been determined. Certainly, he had plenty of opportunities to observe similar characters in his years as a river boat pilot and during his next years spent in the West.

Probably, during the weeks of May and into June, he revised and rewrote the 400 pages he had originally brought with him to Quarry Farm. Applying his idea for the plot he was developing in his mind, he saw that he must discard some of his work and that some needed to be completely redone. He wanted to work toward a use of the cave, but during these early weeks he may have been inspired with several ideas, most of which he discarded.

Depending upon inspiration and having only a sketchy outline for a possible direction to his plot, he wrote steadily during the first weeks of his stay in Elmira, amidst the constant interruptions that family life brings. Much of his writing had to be done in spurts. The manuscript's first sixteen chapters, or 400 plus pages, developed quickly once he had decided upon most of the plot's elements. Here, however, dependent on inspirations he seemed to become snagged again. Writing in spurts, finding solutions to his problems, he worked forward more gradually, rewriting portions and going back to the earlier written parts to make minor changes, many made necessary as the plot developed further.

At certain times, as he recollected various incidents from his years as a boy in Hannibal, or other ideas he believed might fit into his tale, he made notations regarding these on the edges of his manuscript's pages. A few of these he developed, most he forgot or discarded. Sticking with the idea of using the pirates and the cave, he developed the episodes of the raft and the island, producing some of the finest writing in the novel.

All the time he wrote, he continued to envision the creation of a work of uncertain satire, a long "adult" novel aimed at the subscription market served by his publisher. The boyhood of Tom Sawyer was to be only the beginning of this novel. He had plans to extend the adventures of his hero past boyhood into manhood, far past the childish adventures. He knew at this point that he would have to soon reintroduce the theme of the robber villain, whose murder of the doctor in the cemetery at midnight had furnished the blood pact established between Tom and Huck, one patterned after a belief among boys of how confederates operated. Searching for fresh inspiration, he struggled along, trying to overcome interruptions. During this time, possibly, he began to work on the next part of his manuscript, building up to the court room proceedings through more boyhood adventures, developing thoughts about the cloak and dagger sequence. This was to be built around the various burlesqued elements in the cheap, formula novels.

The interruptions to his work were caused by not only the snags in his plotting, but a mixture of unrelated matters. Early in May 1874 he learned that an important character he had created in the novel *The Gilded Age*, the glib "Colonel Sellers," was being used by a clever actor in San Francisco as the basis for a comic stage presentation. Mark Twain, for much of the remaining weeks of that summer, found himself variously involved in the details of the use of legal action and persuasion as he bought off the actor and the writer who had put the script together. Meanwhile, he worked to secure an agreement with Warner so that each of the coauthors might retain the dramatic rights to those characters each had developed. He also spent "a month" rewriting the playwright's original script, according to claims he made to his friend Howells; but it was not a complex play and used dialogue largely drawn from the novel itself. It is thus difficult to determine just how much Twain contributed in terms of dramatic revisions, and how much was the work of the playwright. In addition, the play required that some time be spent obtaining a producer, after which it was readied quickly for presentation on the New York stage in early September.

There are no indications that the interruptions brought about by the play did anything much to hinder the writing being done on *Tom Sawyer*. They may have aided by filling many of those hours when the novel's plot refused to move forward, bridging those periods with creative requirements that helped the author to sustain a high-level creative activity throughout the summer.

During the same months, he was also writing independent sketches and articles as *Tom Sawyer* wore on him and had to be rested. One was a sketch that was written nearly verbatim from the lips of an old woman cook at Quarry Farm that spring. This was to be published in the November issue of that year's *Atlantic* under the title "A True Story," one of his finest pieces of writing. It was the author's first published contribution to the prestigious magazine edited by his friend, William Dean Howells.

About the time he heard and wrote down the story told by the cook, his wife gave birth to their second daughter, Clara, on June 8th. Livy, frail and sickly, always going from one illness to another, was unable to nurse the child and a succession of wet nurses had to be located, interviewed, and hired.

Late in June of 1874, putting aside his concerns for his wife and baby, he interrupted his stay at Quarry Farm and returned to Hartford. This trip took from ten days to almost two weeks from his otherwise busy schedule.

The principle reason for making the trip was to settle the constant quarrels that had arisen between the builder and the architect of the new house, which had been under construction for almost a year. Twain was greatly disturbed when the disagreements between the two threatened to delay completion of the elaborate structure. The trip also allowed attention to be given to certain other matters, some personal and some business, possibly including making some of the arrangements related to the *Colonel Sellers* play.

After returning to Elmira again, near mid-July, he remained at Quarry Farm until August, at which time he and his wife made a short journey to Fredonia, N.Y., where they visited with the author's mother and sister, then residing there. In Fredonia he became involved in a matter that annoyed him greatly and left him with an oppressed disposition for days. Later, after the couple returned to Elmira, Twain reported to Howells that Livy was in a "dreadfully broken down condition" which was to cause them a delay in their plans for immediately traveling back to Hartford.

Between these interruptions, during the hours of that single summer, he managed to find the necessary time and inspiration to compose most of the remaining chapters for *Tom Sawyer*. The work required constant revisions, writing many pages that were revised and thrown away, and the rearranging of certain chapters.

It was probably only in the last weeks of that summer, sometime between mid-July and early September, that he made use of his recollections of how he had as a boy attended picnics near the cave in Hannibal. This allowed him to devise the picnic incident and a reason to place Tom into the cave near "St. Petersburg." Being thoroughly inspired again, he wrote one of the most moving passages of the entire novel, the scenes depicting Tom and Becky lost in the darkness of the cave. This part of the novel may have developed out of his having at one time learned of some boys' becoming lost in one of Hannibal's smaller, lesser known caves — even having passed news of these reports to the Hartford papers through his neighbor, Charles Dudley Warner, editor of Hartford's *Courant*. The fate of those boys would have stuck with him as he, in boyhood, must have explored some of those same formations.

Although he made a claim, at one time, to having been temporarily lost in Hannibal's main cave while on an outing with a young lady friend, there has never been any evidence to confirm his statement and it is usually considered a fanciful statement supplied upon demand, as certain other of his later statements appear also to be. While the first half of *Tom Sawyer* is fiction derived from many actual incidents in the author's boyhood, the last half of the novel is almost entirely straight, invented fiction. Tom and Becky's journey into the cave; the gruesome, though reasonable, death of the villain, Injun Joe; the recovery of the treasure of the thieves after Tom and Huck return to the cave — all these are derived from the author's vivid imagination.

Once again, after Twain had managed to create and to write most of the story to this point, probably sometime in mid-August, his inspiration began to fail him again. As the summer of Tom and Huck was ending, so was his own and he began making plans to return to Hartford. Once more he had to put his manuscript aside. He was then at a point at which he believed he had told less than half of the story he expected to write, having produced only half of what he saw as necessary for a subscription marketed book.

He had hoped to have reached a proper spot from which to send out a matured hero, now freshly supplied with wealth from his treasure find. The author, however, may have been disturbed that he had brought Tom Sawyer through only the childhood depicted in one excessively distorted summer, to a point at which the hero had but partially matured. He was uncertain whether to go on and follow his original idea for writing about an adult hero, or to continue with a young hero. But he was also disturbed about another development that had taken place in his manuscript. Huckleberry Finn, having risen from being a secondary character, had grown in importance — in importance not only to the story, but to his creator.

Sometime, shortly before September work on *Tom Sawyer* came to a complete halt, Twain became once again aware that he would need additional inspiration before the book could "finish itself." He had strong intentions and hopes that he might continue on the manuscript once the family was resettled in their newly constructed house in Hartford. In a letter written to a friend, a doctor in Scotland, he admitted that his inspiration had dried up again and his summer's work remained unfinished.

Twain had, during that summer, probably in two long productive stretches, added another 400 pages of manuscript material to that he had started with. This made his work a manuscript of some 800 pages. It now consisted of 118 pages from the original work of 1872, rescued with some minor revisions; another 107 and some pages completely rewritten from the 1872 material and extended by another 250 pages as a result of work done during April and May 1874 — these together with some 300 to 400 pages that derived from the summer stretch of that year. This is typical of the way in which he wrote, producing pages in haste when fired with inspiration, sometimes writing, according to him, fifty pages a day for stretches. Then when he bogged down, he put the manuscript aside for awhile, and came back to it at a later date, rewriting, revising, and often throwing large sections of manuscript away. It was a method that he had himself explained in a letter written in 1873. There he described the difference between his manner of working and that of Warner during their writing the manuscript for *The Gilded Age*. "Have written many chapters twice, & some three times — have thrown away 300 clean pages of Ms & still there's havoc to be made when I enter on final polishing. Warner has been more forunate — he won't lose 50 pages," the author explained.

Early in September the family packed their possessions and began the trip back to Hartford. He packed the manuscript for *Tom Sawyer* along with his other work. He wanted to put it out of his mind for awhile, unaware that it was actually close to being completed as it would be published. His first thoughts now were of making the play, *Colonel Sellers*, a success. The family stopped over in New York, where Twain lent a hand to the producer and helped to shape the play in the final days before it opened. He was also aware that the new house they were hoping to move into was still unfinished. The family had to move into rooms in the upper stories of the house while work continued on the other parts.

Twain was also very much aware that there was a real need to increase his income, for the house was putting heavier than expected demands on his financial reserves. The need to finish and publish another book must have dominated many of his hours of thought. He needed to write and publish not only for his financial concerns, but for additional prestige. One temporary answer came during October when he received approval from Howells to begin writing a series of sketches for the *Atlantic*, the "Old Times on the Mississippi" series to be based on his piloting days. The writing of this series took up many of his creative hours over the winter months. Although the income he derived from them was minimal, they did manage to keep his name in front of a large and influential body of readers. He occasionally found time to get out his *Tom Sawyer* manuscript to read parts to the family and to hope that he might find the necessary inspiration to go on with the work, but it appears that all he could have been able to add during those months were a couple of chapters of minor importance, one even incorporating pasted-in material clipped from an obscure book.

His money problems were relieved when *Colonel Sellers* proved to be a financial success, although it managed to add little if anything to his literary status. All the while, however, during the months of the winter of 1874–1875, he was aware that this source of income would not continue.

Twain and his wife overextended their financial resources in building the fine house they now lived in, and which they now had to maintain. Meanwhile, the country continued a slide into a period of poor economic conditions. The pressure to create writing that would supply the income he needed continued to grow as the weeks of that winter passed, but he remained uncertain if he would go on with *Tom Sawyer* at some later date, or would discard it and begin work on other things.

# 3. Disappointment and Decision (1875)

In the volumes of *Mark Twain, A Biography*, Albert Bigelow Paine described Mark Twain's summer of 1874 at Quarry Farm in idealistic terms. "There were days, mainly Sundays, when he did not work at all; peaceful days of lying fallow, dreaming in shady places, drowsily watching litttle Susy, or reading with Mrs. Clemens." Speaking of Twain's brother-in-law, Paine reported, "They had portable-hammock arrangements, which they placed side by side on the lawn, and read and discussed through summer afternoons."

Without doubt, the author found some moments to relax but they were probably scarcer than the biographer indicates. Paine does describe a specially constructed outdoor study to which Twain regularly retreated in order to get most of his writing done. "He worked steadily there that summer. He would go up mornings, after breakfast, remaining until nearly dinner-time, say until five o'clock or after, for it was not his habit to eat luncheon."

Far different were the working conditions Twain found when the family returned to Hartford and moved into their new house. Workmen were still busily hammering and sawing, some painting, some moving in furnishings. They would continue to do so for weeks, even months to come. Guests frequently dropped in to visit, the children were a distraction for various reasons, the servants and Mrs. Clemens scurried about, and the author was obligated to face a variety of domestic decisions whenever available. Twain quickly learned to leave the house and go to a room above the stables in order to do any serious thinking and creative writing. Although several of the rooms in the new house had been designed especially for his needs, he seldom could find in them the conditions he needed for his writing.

Ideal working conditions are seldom realized by most authors, even the more fortunate, except for limited periods. Among authors, Mark Twain probably had more than a fair share of extraneous problems to cope with from day to day. One persisting concern was the health of his wife, which varied from fair to critical during most of their years together. During 1875, Mrs. Clemens' health was in such a poor state as to prevent the family from considering traveling to Elmira for the summer. The author's own health, and that of his two daughters, added to the problems, allowing only a month's seaside vacation in August that year.

More important, the growing financial burden of the new house and the family's great desire to entertain everyone who would come to

visit, provoked Twain to serious thoughts about his income. This was intensified by the fact that he had not published a book in over two years.
Evidence, supplied chiefly by his letters, indicates that as the winter
months ended and spring began, he was concerned about his literary
output, but undecided about which way to proceed. "The spring laziness
is already upon me — insomuch that the spirit begins to move me to cease
from Mississippi articles & everything else & give myself over to idleness
until we go to New Orleans," he wrote Howells in late April. The trip
was abandoned, partly because Howells turned down the invitation to
accompany him. Thoughts of beginning a book about the river
remained, but became less prominent. It became a struggle to complete
the series he was writing for the *Atlantic*. The seventh and last of the articles, also the most poorly done, took the longest and was not finished
until June.

His publisher, meanwhile, was preparing to issue a book of
sketches. It had been accepted primarily to keep it from other publishers.
By publishing this volume, composed of unlikely material for a subscription market book, Elisha Bliss also hoped to keep Mark Twain's name
before the public, at least until the author could finish a major work.
Grasping for whatever aid he might receive at that time, Twain entertained occasional expectations that this book, culled from several years
of published material, might furnish enough financial help to tide him
over until he could finish a longer book, one to satisfy the publisher and
be attractive to his readers.

Sometime, during these months, he began again to think of his *Tom
Sawyer* manuscript. He had now put more than a summer's work into it,
yet it was at this point far short of the length usually suited to a
subscription-type book. He was aware that it was not nearly so polished
as he would have liked it to be. His dilemma only grew as he thought
about the problems. Sometime during June, thinking of adding more
chapters to carry it to the original conclusion he had planned — an aging
hero's return to his hometown — he wrote at least a couple of new chapters, intent on lengthening the manuscript — yet the necessary spurt of
enthusiasm continued to elude him.

Realizing that he needed help to decide the fate of his manuscript,
Twain turned to Howells. In mid-June his friend managed a weekend
visit to Hartford. Time prevented Howells from having more than a
brief look at the manuscript. The author urgently sought advice about
it. Following a short but courteous examination of the work, Howells
praised it, even though Twain freely admitted that the story had "no
plot" and tended to "drift." Seeking a way to make a use of the
manuscript, Twain hinted that it might serve as a series of sketches in
the *Atlantic*. Howells, while he had praised the writing, also perplexed
its author, telling him that it would make a good boy's story. This must
have particularly rankled Twain. While he had worked on the material
he had always intended it to be for his almost exclusively adult readers.

Howells' comments, rather than resolving anything for the author,
left him in an even deeper quandary. Twain sensed he had only limited

options. He perhaps could add a more mature theme, or he could abandon the work in favor of another. Still thinking in terms of a "Mississippi
book," he told Howells the new work would use the first person, unlike
*Tom Sawyer*'s use of the third person. This was an intimation of what
became *Huckleberry Finn*, using the character that had grown in importance while working on *Tom Sawyer*—begun from parts of the last
chapters intended for that book and later put aside. Twain had neither
the time nor the inspiration to have produced the remaining half of *Tom
Sawyer* in 1875.

Writing Twain in early July, Howells urged that he begin work on a
new novel, to make it his "chief work," and not to "waste it on a *boy*."
Then, if the *Atlantic* might have the opportunity to publish such a novel,
the editor assured the author its publisher would take all possible legal
action against any newspaper that attempted to copy it. It is evident that
Twain had expressed some fears about infringement of his rights and loss
of profits if unauthorized serial publication in a newspaper preceded
publication as a book. At that moment he was smarting from the recent
knowledge that a Canadian firm, Belford Brothers of Toronto, had
pirated the series of sketches that had appeared in the *Atlantic*. It was
the sort of a risk, however, that he needed to consider because of his dire
need to increase his income.

In a letter to Howells on July 5, Twain stated he was "finished" with
the *Tom Sawyer* manuscript. He told the editor he no longer had any intentions of taking his hero beyond boyhood. He insisted, in direct opposition to Howells' criticism, that what he had written was "*not* a boy's
book." He explained for Howells, "It will only be read by adults. It is
only written for adults." In spite of his great desire to be done with the
work on the manuscript, he told Howells he intended to add another 100
pages to the "about 900 pages of MS" to clear up the "vague places."
While there seemed to be some hope lingering that Howells might yet
consider it for the *Atlantic*, he sensed that Howells was set against doing
so, so he told the editor he believed that publication as a serial by that
magazine would not pay him what he thought the work was worth. He
explained to Howells, "You see I take a vile, mercenary view of things—
but then my household expenses are something almost ghastly." As a
final thought, he asked the editor to read *Tom Sawyer* more thoroughly
"& point out the most glaring defects." He, however, only halfway expected his friend would be willing to grant him the favor.

Howells, replying almost immediately, probably surprised Twain:
"Send on your Ms. when it's ready." Howells made this promise as a
friend, yet he was habitually very polite, and it may have been partly
done in placation since he had had to agree with Twain that the *Atlantic*
would not run the work, especially for the price Twain seemed to
suggest it was worth. Howells, however, again expressed his genuine interest in the pending novel the author was contemplating.

For some reason, Twain had meanwhile decided to attempt a new
tactic. On July 13 he wrote Howells: "Just as soon as you consented I
realized all the atrocity of my request, & straightway blushed &

weakened. I telegraphed my theatrical agent to come here & carry off the MS & copy it." Then the author followed with a suggestion that Howells might take the story and dramatize it. This suggestion Howells turned down, politely but quickly, on July 19, telling the author: "I couldn't do it, and if I could, it wouldn't be a favor to dramatize your story. In fact I don't see how anybody can do that but yourself. I could never find the time for one thing." It was a delicate statement, one that Twain must have read over several times, probably uncertain as to its intent.

As Twain came to realize there appeared to be little hope for publication of his manuscript, either as a serial or a book, he began to hope that somehow he might earn something for the efforts he had expended on the material by turning it into a dramatic work. Often when a thought such as this struck him, he immediately began working on it. On July 21 he submitted a synopsis of his story to the Library of Congress for a dramatic copyright, calling it "TOM SAWYER, A Drama." A most significant factor about this synopsis, written at least a few days previously, if not earlier, is that it incompasses almost all of what would make up the published book. This indicates perhaps that all the essential work had been done ten months earlier.

The conditions prevailing make it almost certain he could not have completed the last half of his novel, especially as some of it is the finest fiction writing of his entire career, in the time he had available and certainly not in the state of mind he was in, deliberating whether to go on with the work or to abandon it. The last two paragraphs of this synopsis can be cited as evidence that, smarting as he was under Howells' criticism of it as a boy's story, he had attempted to develop a more mature plot line. It also reveals the importance that Huck Finn had assumed in the considerations going on in his perplexed mind. The first of these two paragraphs states:

> Tom takes Huck to cave; they dig under figure of the cross, and get the treasure. Widow Douglas takes Huck into her family, and distresses the life out of the vagabond with her cleanly, systematic, and pious ways. He, Tom, and Joe Harper turn robbers, and so make use of the cave.

The last sentence in this indicates that the author planned to continue with his "blood and thunder" satire and intended to center its action about the cave. Had Twain not already developed the last chapters of *Tom Sawyer*, he would not have written such a thorough synopsis, for it was not often he would proceed to outline material so much in actual detail before he wrote it out. It also tends to suggest that his manuscript included one or more chapters which Twain had done in this period of June 1875 but which were later to be largely removed from the published book. The similarity to the opening pages of *Huckleberry Finn* is obvious in the last sentence.

The second, concluding paragraph in this revealing synopsis shows that Twain still had thoughts about his original plan for a long novel. It indicates clearly that his manuscript had not developed beyond the point indicated in the paragraph above and also that he knew he would need to make an enormous leap in the story to handle the transposition to the intended conclusion, one still undeveloped in his mind. Deciding upon the sparse wording of a single sentence, in the final paragraph he describes his goal: "FIFTY YEARS LATER. — Ovation to General Sawyer, Rear-Admiral Harper, Bishop Finn, and Inspectator Sid Sawyer, the celebrated detective." While the possibilities of continuing and then ending the story in this fashion would be limitless, the story also would invite treatment as a burlesque. There seems little doubt that the author had not yet faced the problems of envisioning a detailed history of the characters he mentions. If nothing else, this conclusion of the dramatic synopsis reveals the author's dilemma in those matters concerning the unstable condition and value of his manuscript, especially as a publishable item.

The summer of 1875 surely must have been continually upsetting to Twain's ambitions as he seemed only to be marking time. His literary output reached a low point and his attempts to do something effective with the manuscript for *Tom Sawyer* seem to have gained nothing. The entire summer was a disappointment, with Livy being ill much of the time, with the children often sick, and with Twain himself going through periods in which one or another ailment upset his normally good health. As usually happened when he could not be creative in a literary way, he undertook other pursuits, putting extensive efforts into the problems relating to copyright laws for a while, a matter he believed seriously affected his income. When not fretting about the copyright laws, he managed to involve himself in a variety of minor business affairs. Though the expense of operating the new house continued to grow, he remained reluctant to cut back the family's budget. Yet, it was a year of poor economic conditions. His previously published books were not then selling well, and the need to publish another continued to haunt him. The reception accorded the publication of *Sketches, New and Old* after it had appeared in September indicated that it obviously would not serve that need.

Possibly somewhat peeved, if not resentful, because of the lack of interest he believed Howells had shown in *Tom Sawyer*, Twain spent several months during which he made no other efforts to approach the editor about the work. Not until late in the fall would he again look to his friend for help with it. This accompanied another event, one which has never been clearly understood — the acceptance of the *Tom Sawyer* manuscript by Mark Twain's publisher, the American Publishing Company of Hartford. While there is no positive evidence of what happened, it could have been that events were similar to those surrounding the *Sketches* book. On February 12, in a letter to James R. Osgood, Twain indicated he had originally planned to let Osgood be the publisher of that work. He then noted that when Elisha Bliss, who directed most of the affairs of the American Publishing Company, learned about the

Osgood offer, Bliss went to an office safe and "brought back a contract *four years* old to give him all my old sketches, with a lot of new ones added!"

Although Twain was able to call Bliss "the old fox," it was a case of either the author's having forgotten about the existence of the contract or, more likely, his having hoped that Bliss had discarded it or forgotten about it. The contract existed in the first place in order for Bliss to keep other publishers from getting any book length work by Mark Twain, although the *Sketches* book was not typical subscription market material. Bliss, a sharp businessman with a keen eye for profits, knew that Twain was his best selling author and wanted, if possible, to maintain that advantage. While Twain may appear to have been fretting to Osgood in his letter, he must have been pleased that the matter had at least resulted in a promise that the *Sketches* book would be taken on by what then was the leading subscription publisher in the country.

As Twain had that summer apparently moved away from a serious interest in writing because he was not in the best of his creative moods, he also appears to have given little attention, if any, to the reading of the proof sheets for the *Sketches* book. Meanwhile, the matter of the fate of *Tom Sawyer* remained unresolved, the author having no clear inspiration about it. He may have even begun to push it to the back of his mind. However, the dismal results forecast early for sales of the *Sketches* book perhaps prompted him to do something about finishing the novel. He may have concluded the work should be published in a form close to that in which it then stood, even though it was still a long way from the story he had set out to write. He now recalled having told Howells earlier he was "finished" with the manuscript, vague as his thinking was regarding the story's ending and its real value as a book. Osgood, the records show, was only one of many publishers always eager to receive any sort of manuscript written by Twain. Around this time the author undoubtedly recalled a letter containing a request for a book length manuscript he had received earlier that year, and rejected, on the same day he had written Osgood about the earlier signed contract with Bliss.

H.O. Houghton, head of the firm of Hurd & Houghton, as well as publisher of the *Atlantic*, had written the author in hopes of getting a manuscript for a series of "bright, short American novels" which Hurd & Houghton was then publishing. Twain's rejection of the offer was basically because of the "money side of it." He recalled it now as he discovered a greater need for money and at the same time was reaching a decision that *Tom Sawyer* could serve in its present length as the type of manuscript suitable for Houghton's firm. At this point, somehow, whether accidently or purposefully, the matter came to the attention of Elisha Bliss. When it did, the publishing executive once again went to his safe and produced another contract, from 1872, made up for a book on the diamond mines of South Africa, a book which never got to the writing stage, principally because it was to have been created from notes to have been furnished by a newspaper reporter friend who died before they were completed. Also, the author had obviously lost interest in the book. Again, we do not know if Twain realized that Bliss was still holding the contract (although an advance had been paid on behalf of the book and never was returned by the author), but surely the publisher once again made it plain to the author that the American Publishing Company would not permit any other firm to publish a book length work by Mark Twain so long as an unfulfilled contract existed.

As there was no new contract written to cover *Tom Sawyer*'s publication and later evidence shows clearly that this contract was applied to the novel, something on this order decided the book's fate. Once more, knowing that the work would be handled by the publisher of his choice, the best subscription house, Twain eagerly turned the manuscript over to Bliss. Hopeful about it, he now told Bliss that he expected the firm would issue the novel in the spring of 1876.

There is no written evidence of what actually happened, but the above seems as reasonable and likely a description of what occurred as any that can be built on the available evidence. Whatever did happen, it is known that the manuscript, or a part of it, was in the hands of Bliss on November 5, at which time Twain wrote to him, "You may let Williams have all of Tom Sawyer that you have received." The author was referring to True Williams, the illustrator for *Tom Sawyer*. It is possible that Twain may have retained the last couple of chapters of his manuscript while hoping to find a more conclusive and satisfactory ending. He probably was not having further thoughts about lengthening the work. Undoubtedly, Twain was having second thoughts about the work, whatever they were, perhaps that it was not worthy of the efforts he had put into it.

Twain added in his November 5, 1875, letter to Bliss, "[Williams] wants it, and I have not the least objection, because if he should lose any of it I have got another complete MS copy." This letter was written shortly after Twain sent the "copy" manuscript to Howells. This indicates a fresh dilemma regarding the novel had arisen, since the prospects of its being published were now very good. Twain sent Howells the manuscript on October 27, writing, "Say boss, do you want this to lighten up your old freight train with? I suppose you won't but then it won't take you long to say so." His excuse for not including return postage was that he did not have the necessary stamps available. It appears a lame explanation.

# 4. Problems of Publication (1875–1876)

The acceptance of the *Tom Sawyer* manuscript by the American Publishing Company was an important step. However, problems remained for Mark Twain and the publisher. The author remained troubled over the book's brief length, uneasy about its lack of a strong plot, and unsure of certain parts of the material he had included. The concluding chapters were of particular concern. Less visible, but hanging over all this, were Howells' words that the work would primarily interest boy readers. This left him deeply depressed.

Twain had customarily written for an adult audience, aiming at them his humor and satire intentionally laden with moral messages. Even as a young printer, in the very beginning of his career in Hannibal, what he wrote was mainly directed toward adults. In fact, in almost every instance his work is directed at universal audiences — the finest of his writing being deeper and more serious than his enormous reputation as a popular humorist suggests.

Although time would bring him to compromise his opinion that *Tom Sawyer* would "only be read by adults," Twain would face and resolve the problems that arose with the publisher with less luck and less grace. Governed by his own motives, Elisha Bliss followed a series of delay tactics of which the author seemed hardly aware at times. When Twain was convinced he had succeeded in requesting the publisher to prepare and issue *Tom Sawyer* for the "early spring market," Bliss apparently had no intention of publishing another book by the author until a time that was most opportune for the company. When the author asked Bliss to pursue English publishers for publication in that market, Bliss did little or nothing to help. There may be some possibility that Bliss' early inaction resulted from the author's own divided and uncertain feelings about the novel, for Bliss had a shrewd businessman's insight. Surely Bliss would have noted that while Twain was urging the publisher forward, he himself was unsure of his work.

After Howells completed a reading of the copy manuscript the author had sent him for a more studied opinion, he replied to him in a letter written November 21. The author's close friend again praised the story, but again he also emphasized that it was "altogether the best boy's story I ever read." Howells explained, "I have made some corrections and suggestions in faltering pencil, which you'll have to look for." Most of these notations were done in regard to the early chapters of the book, the part that had derived from the early sketch-like material. Howells then added, "…I don't seem to think I like the last chapter. I believe I would cut that." This was perhaps what Twain feared he would hear. He wrote Howells dejectedly, "Just send Sawyer to me by Express — I enclose money for it. If it should get lost it will be no great matter."

Mark Twain sometimes would ease the difficulty of making an important decision by not making it himself, but instead take it to his wife, Livy, for her opinion. He replied to Howells, "Mrs. Clemens decides with you that the book should issue as a book for boys, pure and simple — & so do I." While this suggests that he had capitulated to Howells' criticism and to his wife's confirmation of that criticism, it really did little to change his lagging enthusiasm for the *Tom Sawyer* manuscript. Twain now found himself in a more depressed mood than before. During the next six weeks he had a series of illnesses. If not caused by his distressed mood, they were at least not ameliorated by it. When the manuscript was received back, the author put it aside, completely ignoring it and his friend's suggestions until early in January of 1876.

It was essentially the continuing need to bolster his income that caused Twain to write Howells a note at the start of the new year for the purpose of inquiring if the editor might still welcome some new contributions for the *Atlantic*. Howells replied affirmatively. "We were both — Mrs. Howells and I — getting up a bad state of feeling toward you both, because you hadn't made any sign of existence for so long...." Twain wrote back, "Indeed we haven't forgotten the Howellses, nor scared up a grudge of any kind against them; but the fact is I was under the doctor's hands for four weeks on a stretch, & have been disabled from working for a week or so beside." The use of the emphatic tone in this denial tends to confirm the existence of tensions. The interest of the author in *Tom Sawyer* was suddenly being renewed. The prominent part that money played in the author's revived considerations must not be overlooked.

By early in January, in addition to the kind remarks Howells had made about *Tom Sawyer* again when he inquired about its progress, Twain had had a look at the drawings Williams had done for the illustrations in the novel. The author reported then to Howells as "about 200 rattling pictures." Following a visit by Moncure D. Conway, an American preacher working in England, the author answered a note concerning the whereabouts of Conway's overshoes by asking his recent guest to come back and consider taking a copy of the *Tom Sawyer* manuscript to England when making the return voyage. Having thought about the plan and perhaps having checked with the reluctant Bliss to learn if anything had been done about finding a publisher in England for the work, Twain apparently concluded that he would pursue certain suggestions that had come from Conway.

Although when writing Bliss two months earlier he had claimed to have received a tentative offer of a contract from Routledge & Sons, the English publisher who had brought out his earlier books, to publish *Tom Sawyer* (or more than likely just the author's *next* book, since they had not seen the manuscript), he had not answered them because, as now became obvious, he was seeking a method whereby he might retain a

HUCKLEBERRY FINN.

BECKY THATCHER

AUNT POLLY.

*Of these drawings by True W. Williams, 161 were used in the American first edition of* Tom Sawyer. *The idyllic picture of Tom, upper left, faced the title page. Other examples, depicting leading characters, show, clockwise, Huckleberry Finn, Williams' version of Aunt Polly, and Becky Thatcher.*

*Evidence of what Twain told Howells in his January 18, 1876, letter: "I finally concluded to cut the Sunday-school speech down to the first two sentences...." In the upper left corner of this page 89 of the original manuscript Twain jotted down an idea for naming a steamboat, "City of Hartford," used in an earlier written sketch but not in* Tom Sawyer. *(Courtesy of the Georgetown University Library).*

a greater share of the book's earnings than normally offered. Making this line of thought necessary was the pressure he was experiencing on his income — so, under the new circumstance, his hope once more restored, Twain briefly returned to work on the *Tom Sawyer* manuscript, essentially making some of the changes which Howells had suggested in the penciled notations.

In several of the most detailed paragraphs in evidence which describe work done on the manuscript, Twain wrote Howells on January 18 that he had put himself "to the dreary & hateful task of making final revision of Tom Sawyer." He told in his letter of opening the package containing the copy manuscript, hunting out the notations made by Howells, then making "the emendations which they suggested." He cut a long section concerning a "boy-battle to a curt paragraph...." He cut a Sunday-school speech "down to the first two sentences...." He reduced the satire of the book, noting that "the book is to be for boys & girls...." He then added that he had "tamed the various obscenities..." (none being any obscenities in the modern sense). All told, he wrote that he had finished in a "single setting" revisions that would have required "3 or 4 days," and which would have left him "mentally & physically fagged out at the end."

If the changes were made in a single setting, as the author stated, then he worked long and hard that day, for there were several important decisions made affecting the texture of the novel, decisions that required thought and the application of a talented mind. Most were decisions that pertained to which of Howells' suggestions would be adopted either wholly or in part, or not at all. Especially important to the tone of the book were those various suggestions followed concerning crudities both of words and phrases. The author's corrections here are noticeable improvements. These revisions made at this "single setting," some which required the rewriting of small sections, put the story into its final, published form. Only one small change was apparently made later by the author in the American edition during the proof reading process. It was the knowledge that Conway was coming to take a copy of the manuscript with him that undoubtedly inspired Twain to perform this intensive series of last minute revisions on the work, which he reported on to Howells.

While Twain had the *copy* manuscript before him when he made the revisions, we do not know whether he also had all of the *original* with him at this time. Most of those revisions done at this time were apparently done first on the *copy* manuscript, then applied to those parts of the *original* he had retrieved from the publisher. It appears that here, as well as earlier, he made efforts to produce manuscripts that agreed; but, he succeeded only in a limited fashion. That his attempts to make the two manuscripts agree were not perfect can be readily noticed when the English edition, whose type was set from the *copy*, is compared to the American edition, done from the *original*. Certain differences are a direct result of Twain's not being thorough in transposing the material as he revised his manuscripts. There are a number of other differences that

may be laid to the carelessness of the typesetters, some perhaps a result
of the varied customs of language and punctuation between the British
and American usages and habits regarding English. These secondary
variations account for approximately 150 differences of various sorts.
While the sum total of all differences between the two editions, with
minor exceptions, does not have any appreciable effect upon the story itself, they strongly suggest a lack of artistic, or literary interest, which the
author seems to have had in the novel at this time, compared to the apparently strong commercial concerns that were influencing him. Also, to
an extent, it is still another indication of the haphazard way in which
Twain performed much of the creative labor he gave to his longer
works. This was a manner of working not so much deliberate as it was
the result of a mind that could concentrate brilliantly on individual
words, sentences, and often on separate units of a book, but could not
seem to visualize the entire work with the necessary clarity to
homogeneously manage its overall development.

What might be considered an equal fault, one about which Twain
continually deluded himself, was the small ability he owned to take the
business matters of publishing into his own hands. His successes as an
author are an obvious contrast to his failures as a businessman. This
point, illustrated in many areas of his career, is amply illustrated in the
history of the publication of *Tom Sawyer*. His decision to handle the
matter of publication of *Tom Sawyer* in England on his own, using
Conway as an agent, came about partly because he realized that Bliss
was doing nothing to attend to the matter. He had also begun to entertain thoughts that his income from a more controlled type of publication
could be greater. Too, he was very aware that there were clear advantages to be gained in the matter of copyright if the work were to be
published first under the protection of the British Empire laws. Conway,
as he had been requested and because he had several lecture dates to
fulfill, returned to Hartford on January 18 to pick up a copy of the
manuscript, delighted that Twain had selected him to be a courier. No
matter whether the plan had originated with Conway or with the
author, by this point, Twain was as enthusiastic about it as his visitor,
for it would especially enable him to get his hands into the publishing
end.

The scheme that they had decided upon was for Conway to oversee
publication in England by a publisher who would be paid for all the
costs of publication and would take only a royalty on the copies they
sold. It was a complete turnabout of the common practice, an uncommon sort of subsidy publishing. Overlooking its novelty, it had appealed
greatly to Twain as he saw it as a promising answer to his hopes to sub-
stantially boost his earnings. At the same time he believed it to be the
ideal answer to certain of the problems he had had before with
copyrights.

Conway, exhibiting his pleasure in having a part in the publication
of a book by Mark Twain, accepted the opportunity without question.
On the same day he visited the author, Conway wrote home to his wife,

"Mark Twain has written a remarkable book called 'Tom Sawyer,' a book which I wish you to try your hand in preparing the way for negotiations with Chatto [&] Windus." This undertaking, prompting the author's last minute efforts to revise and complete the manuscript, carries a great share of the responsibility for *Tom Sawyer*'s being published as it was. It may also be responsible for that novel's being published at all.

In England, after Mrs. Conway approached Chatto & Windus, they replied in a letter, "We shall be happy to undertake the publication of Mark Twain's new work upon the terms suggested...." Twain was to bear the entire production cost and pay the publisher a 10 per cent royalty upon the total amount of sales, undoubtedly the agreement that the two men had outlined earlier. However, when Conway sailed with the *copy* manuscript on March 11, two days following another visit with Twain, he apparently had instructions to press for better terms from Chatto & Windus, as well as to consult with other publishers. The firm of G. Routledge & Sons, one which Twain seemed to have a preference for as he had already dealt with them, rejected the plan at first but agreed with reluctance to accept its terms after further persuasion. This last, if for no other reason, led Conway to write the author he was "disinclined to let them have Tom Sawyer."

Twain took some pride in his belief that he could efficiently handle business matters. He often made a point of his ability to "cipher," a term defined broadly by him for financial astuteness when complimenting himself. But soon, he began to find that he was becoming "puzzled" by the number of troublesome factors involved in the various offers being forwarded to his attention. Also, it must be noted, that at this time he believed that the American edition was to be issued soon after May 1st and this, consequently left only a short while to allow any English edition to precede it. Another, and an important factor, was that his financial condition, strained to its limits at the time by the slow sale of his books and the expanded cost of maintaining the new house, left the author unable to finance the subsidy plans. He also realized that this condition showed no clear signs of improving in the near future. If he delayed too long while he made arrangements to supply the financing, he foresaw that it could delay the English publication and endanger his copyright strategy. Both English firms, it appears, had offered to publish the novel by the usual method of handling the production cost themselves and paying a standard royalty on sales to the author. Twain found that it was not an easy decision for him to make and again submitted the matter to Livy. She did not hesitate. "Take the royalty; it simplifies everything; removes all risks; requires no outlay of capital; makes the labor easy for Mr. Conway; a gain of 25 per cent profit is hardly worth the trouble and risk of publishing on your own account." Whether or not the decision was the one Twain most desired, it appears to have been the only one open for him.

When he reported the decision to Conway, Twain wrote, "Hardly any of the pictures are finished yet." Although the novel had been set up in type (Howells reading the rough proof sheets sometimes before March 20), the engravings for the illustrations were being delayed, quite possibly by Bliss as a deliberate means to control the time of the work's publication. Twain, being either unwilling or unable to realize this, went on to tell Conway in his letter of April 9 that he believed "the book won't issue till 2 or even 4 weeks" after the appearance of the May issue of the *Atlantic*. In back of this was the fact that Howells was expected to publish his review of the book in that issue to provide it a promotional boost. Though Twain regularly spoke as if he had maintained total control over matters of publication and the order in which they would precede, in truth he had no control whatsoever.

When Twain told Conway to give the book to Chatto & Windus if they were still "willing," he only provided the agent with tentative information, leaving Conway to decide upon a number of matters still unsettled. Some of the items left to Conway's decision were putting in the "preface" or not, or altering it; determining the size and shape of the book; and the matter of the furnishing of the plates to produce an illustrated English edition.

About the time Howells' review was being printed, Twain had to reluctantly admit to Conway that the American edition was to be further delayed. He boasted, "Consequently I have told Bliss to issue in the autumn and make a Boy's Holiday Book of it." More than likely, the author was merely agreeing to an estimate given by Bliss of when the novel was to be issued in America. Further, having finally received confirmation from A.R. Spoffman, Librarian of Congress, of the copyright procedure they were following, he notified Conway, "First publication in England cannot impair my American copyright..." and left to Conway the decision to set the date for English publication with Chatto. With the matter of the illustrations still far from any reasonable resolution (and some of the details about them would require months to resolve), Chatto & Windus made a decision to proceed at once with an English edition of *Tom Sawyer* without the use of illustrations.

Meanwhile, Howells' review appeared with the American publication date still far in the future. This left to Twain the task of explaining the delay to his friend. In a letter to Howells on April 26, he placed the full blame for the delay of publication on Bliss (which in essence may have been very near to the truth), and added, "the engravers assisting, as usual." The remainder of this letter, in regard to *Tom Sawyer*, gives evidence of the continuing series of frustrations that Twain suffered month after month in 1876. Finally, he managed to acknowledge, "Howells, you must forgive me...." As serious as the blunder had been, seeing the review of the book published so far ahead of the publication date, Howells, polite as usual, displayed no obvious concern, and replied to the author, "I rather like the fun of the thing...." It is hard to believe, however, that he did not have some feelings of exasperation for the way his friend was conducting matters.

Bliss, too, may have been upset by Twain's series of "orders," and his meddling, along with other factors, but he seems to have done little or nothing to reveal it to the author. Twain, again spending his summer at Quarry Farm, "booming along" on a new novel (parts of *Huckleberry Finn*), continued to try to do something about the illustrations for the English edition. It was already in production, but this was not known to the author.

Driven by a growing frustration, the author sent some presumptive directives to Bliss, not only about the matter of *Tom Sawyer*, but some regarding general things pertaining to the operations of the American Publishing Company. (Mark Twain had become a director in the firm, though records indicate he rarely attended any board meetings.) In this dark mood, on June 24, he wrote Bliss ostensibly to report that he was ready for the final proof sheets of *Tom Sawyer*, but then continued his letter with a series of unrealistic suggestions for changes in a number of business matters under the control of Bliss. Bliss, probably containing his anger, did not answer the author until mid-July. Then, claiming he had been prevented from answering due to illness, Bliss was able to respond with words somewhat toned down from those he might first have used. Still, the answer was put in terms sufficiently strong to illustrate the amount of displeasure at Twain's suggestions. Twain, quickly retreating from his original position, admitted to having acted "unwisely." The remainder of his reply was limited to a continuing concern over the issuance of *Tom Sawyer*, but it indicates a hope that he might somehow commit the publisher to a publication date for the novel of not later than the first of November.

On August 1, having "received and read" no more than the first eight chapters of the American edition of *Tom Sawyer* in the final proof form (divided into pages and including the illustrations), Twain wrote a long letter to Conway, being still in a quandary regarding the matter of supplying the plates for the English publisher. It shows him as being quite uncomfortable in the mixup of matters between Bliss, the English publisher, and Conway as he sought to bring some order into the affair. He was aware that the English edition had been published by then and may have already received a copy of the actual first edition of his novel, published in London on June 9 without illustrations.

Twain referred to it as the "cheap edition." The matter of the American edition's publication date was still under the control of Bliss, he obviously determined to set it to suit the needs he saw for the company. A classic had been created, but none close to it fully realized what had taken place. The troubled author — continuing to press Bliss to commit himself to a date, meanwhile denying that he was dealing with any other publisher regarding another book — certainly did not seem elated by the event.

# 5. The Troubled Author (1876)

The United States celebrated its 100th anniversary in 1876, a year which saw numerous celebrations about the nation at various times and places, some remembered, most forgotten. One of these events that came late and went by with only slight notice, was the publication of *Tom Sawyer*. There were many reasons for 1876 to have been a happy year, as it was for many people, the Civil War a fading memory, new opportunities for progress existing in the expanding nation—but in many ways life and its problems went on as usual, celebrations aside. If one would have tried to determine that year which of the events occurring would be most recalled after a second hundred years had passed, probably no one would have chose the publication of *Tom Sawyer*.

For Twain, in pursuit of a literary career, 1876 was an uncomfortable year, in spite of its historical significance. It was a disturbing year, the author seemingly plagued by the constant troubles accompanying the publication of *Tom Sawyer*. It was also troublesome in many other ways. His first biographer later hinted strongly that all was not well for Twain at age 40. Twain is quoted bitterly suggesting, "The symbol of the race ought to be a human being carrying an ax, for every human being has one concealed about him somewhere, and is always seeking the opportunity to grind it." A later biographer agreed and stated, "For Mark Twain the spirit of '76 was troubled and divided."

Although in retrospect, it now appears as a pivotal point in the rise of his career as a man of letters, at age 40 Mark Twain was faced with thoughts of his mortality, reminded of this when the beloved uncle of his childhood, John Quarles, died on February 25. He was reminded again that year when his father and brother's bodies were moved to new grave sites in Hannibal. He was concerned about his future, striving to fill the role he had established for himself as a writer of books, foregoing the lecture circuits and aiming at a reputation above that of a popular humorist. He had set his hopes on following *Tom Sawyer* with a bigger and better novel, to fulfill his original plans, but these hopes died as what he termed the "double-barreled novel" was aborted, and "Huck Finn's Autobiography," as he then spoke of that future masterpiece, had accumulated to a typical "400 pages" and was in grave danger of being burned because of his troubled mood. He realized he had to show signs of progress. He had seen himself rise from a childhood state of near poverty to one of comparative wealth and fame—and knew that to maintain this status, not only to improve it, would take even greater efforts than those he had been able to rally.

In a letter to his boyhood friend Will Bowen around this time, Twain chided Bowen for a "pettying & pitying & admiring" sentiment, urging he rid himself of it and say, "'Thanks be to God I have passed my sentimental worms, & have no longer the moral belly-ache'." Obviously, it was a lesson he was himself in the process of learning. Respected as he was as a humorist, Twain did not always see himself as the public saw him. Significant to the state of his mind that year was the bizarre item he had published in the June *Atlantic*, a piece more biting than it was humorous, "The Facts Concerning the Recent Carnival of Crime in Connecticut." In this strange sketch he faced his "Conscience" embodied in a drawf, grotesque "Mark Twain." Observing no other alternative, he puts the all-too-real vision to a violent end, concluding (perhaps punningly) "Since that day my life is all bliss. Bliss, unalloyed bliss. Nothing in all the world could persuade me to have a conscience again."

That same summer, in the hilltop study where the greater part of *Tom Sawyer* had been written he now worked on "1601," a slightly scurrilous piece which was privately printed and circulated only in a limited manner for years. It was again symptomatic of the divided attitude he struggled against, then and for the years to follow. He was at the beginning of his eight year struggle to finish the notable book which was to become the masterpiece of his career, *The Adventures of Huckleberry Finn*. Still, his need for income and public acceptance would cause him to write and publish works of a lesser value in the meantime, because he thought that it was what his public image demanded: *A Tramp Abroad* (1880), in which the citizen of Hartford labels himself a *tramp*; *The Prince and the Pauper* (1882), featuring a *pauper* who through a quirk of fate lives the life of a prince; and *Life on the Mississippi* (1883), devoted to the young river boat pilot who had known a more spirited *life* on the Mississippi. Each of these works features an alternate hero, their divided creator in one of his disguises. By 1876 it was apparent to the author that he had created a role for himself that was greater than his private self.

Twain needed for *Tom Sawyer* to be a commercial success, unsure of how it would be accepted by those who had read his other books, uncertain of what effect it might have upon his career. Already there appear in *Tom Sawyer* traces of the reflections of the darker side of life that were embodied in his philosophical visions. It is a mistake to see it only as a light-hearted boy's book, as Howells first saw it. But even Howells, by the time he had written his ill-timed review, had looked at the work more critically and moved away from that restricting view. In March, Moncure Conway wrote the author thoughtfully, "I don't think it would be doing justice to call it a boy's book and think it better be left people to form their own conclusions...." Then, in long reviews published in England and America, Conway tried to demonstrate some of the depth he saw in Mark Twain's new novel. Elisha Bliss, not a critic, though a perceptive reader, continuing to bide his time toward the publication date of *Tom Sawyer*, when writing the canvassing material for the volume's salespeople, also appears to have shown a heightened opinion

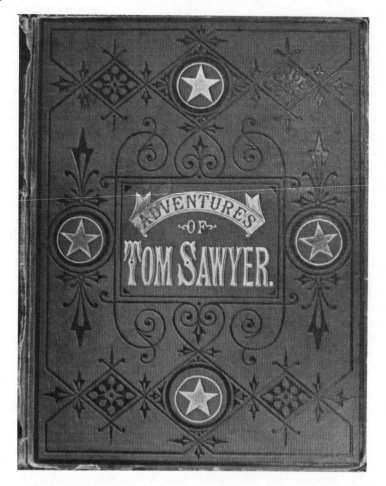

*The ornate design, printed on blue cloth, of the cover of the American Publishing Company's first edition of* The Adventures of Tom Sawyer *was used on all succeeding printings until 1903 when Harper & Bros. took over publication.*

of the work, though what he wrote was for commercial purposes rather than for critical purposes:

> The genius requisite to render the written adventures of a boy over-whelmingly fascinating to grown-up readers, is possessed by few, and challenges the deepest admiration.... No words have seemed too strong to express the pleasure felt at this fresh exhibition of the author's powers, exerted in a direction least expected....

Such an opinion is acceptable today but not a hundred years ago, when the public was just getting acquainted with Twain. While he was pleased with what his friends and associates were saying, he failed to show that he himself had a higher opinion of what he was publishing as he went through with what he considered the dreary task of checking the final proof sheets as they were sent to him by Bliss, his disinterest apparent in the several errors he obviously overlooked. A more certain proof of his assessment of the work can be seen in the fact that, during the summer of 1876, he continued his hopes that the work could be translated into a stage presentation, one strictly along lines that suggest he looked upon it as an opportunity for burlesque themes and performances, an attitude that never seemed to change greatly for him as the novel began to show its appeal to readers of all ages. For today's critic, who sees in *Tom Sawyer* complex and serious themes important to its status as a classic, it may seem strange that the author could have the slighting attitude he had for the book.

The American edition's appearance, when it finally came from the publisher on December 8, 1876, was almost anticlimactic. It followed the English publication by several months, a matter that had itself caused the author many moments of anguish as he fumbled with difficult decisions. From this publication came the pirated edition published in Canada that led to still more severe anguish, striking at the heart of one of the problems that he concerned himself with during many hours, weak copyright laws which robbed a writer of some of the wages of his labor. Although greatly angered by this act of piracy and desperately wanting to strike back at the pirates, he found that he lacked both the means and the full cooperation of those that he appealed to for aid.

Considering the many problems that the publication of the American edition had endured, it must have brought a genuine sigh of relief to the author, if only a momentary relief, for the reviews it received were few and none were encouraging. The first sales figures, too, were discouraging to the author who had seen the novel as a fair chance to do away with many of the financial concerns that he faced. Twain's expressed hope that *Tom Sawyer* might outsell all of his other books (written to that time) remained a matter for future years to realize.

Five days after the date of the American edition's publication, Twain wrote Moncure Conway. He then seemed unaware of the long-range value of his novel, unaware it would remain in print and continue to sell for his lifetime, that when the Bicentennial Celebrations would occur a hundred years hence it would be ranked by many as his second best book, ranked by some critics as his "best constructed" novel, and that Tom Sawyer would become one of the most widely recognized characters in American literature. Certainly not aware, and surely unconcerned that *The Adventures of Tom Sawyer* would become a familiar classic, in one of his many dark moods, he explained to Conway: "It is a mistake, I am not writing any new book. Belford [the Canadian pirate publisher] has taken the profits all out of 'Tom Sawyer.' We find our copyright law here to be nearly worthless, and if I can make a living out of plays, I shall never write another book."

It was surely not a fitting way in which to conclude a year that had begun on a hopeful note with high expectation for financial rewards for his novel, or to conclude the long period in which he had labored unsure and uncertain as to what sort of a book he was creating. Although he would never profit again from the writing of a play, he could not have seriously considered that he might never write another book. Writing was itself more important to him than success, whether he realized this or not — and he was to face similar problems for the remaining years of his life, his financial problems diminishing only during the last decade as he struggled to play the role more of a sage than a humorist.

# Part II

## *Background*

# 6. A Book for Boys?

Those who classify *The Adventures of Tom Sawyer* as a mere boy's adventure book ignore certain things about its creation and its creator. The creative resources Mark Twain drew upon for the writing of *Tom Sawyer* represent almost all of the experiences of his life up to that point. A complexity of items both major and minor, scattered throughout his past, furnished recognizable influences on the work. For some of the central parts of the story he sampled the varied and vivid memories he carried, a large number since the early days of his childhood. Some date far back in time to the world he first saw around him in his birthplace, Florida, Missouri. To these were added other memories left from his summer vacations spent there. Over these are laid the extensive and exciting adventures of the boyhood years experienced in Hannibal while growing up.

All these memories needed to be filtered through the training and experience that came with his varied career, first on the river, then in the West, and thereafter as he took his place in the cultured society of the East. First as a printer, then as a pilot, then a miner, and finally as a journalist and a lecturer he developed the tools to handle his experience. To the experience was added the reading of many books. As a result of the fusing of this broad background in the book, *Tom Sawyer* became a novel that contains values for all readers, from the youngest child looking for a likely adventure tale to the serious scholar searching for obscure meanings.

Certain books possess a universal appeal, a unique aura, being read and enjoyed by generations of children and adults alike. They become classics because of some elusive quality, sometimes so fragile and vaporous that it defies an accurate description, which ensnares the readers and draws them into the story like a gentle net. Those who allow *The Adventures of Tom Sawyer* any attention have little doubt that it is among such books.

An array of statistics lend support to the nomination of this novel as a classic. It has longevity, having been continuously in print since 1876. The numerous editions in both the original and foreign languages attest to its broad appeal. In addition, it has suffered the fate of being abridged, turned into several motion pictures, taken apart for numerous dramatic adaptations, and turned into comic books. From the modest sales of its first year it has consistently continued as a marketable item among books until many millions of copies of it now abound in libraries and homes everywhere.

Twain did not regard *Tom Sawyer* as the work he most wished to be remembered for, his personal choice being *Joan of Arc*, his little-read treatment of that popular theme. Critics in general have never considered it as his most valuable contribution to literature, their nomination going almost universally to *Huckleberry Finn*, as it must for good reasons. Still, the numbers who have read and will read *Tom Sawyer* can be said to easily outnumber the readers of any of Twain's other works. It is the most popular book of one of the most popular of American authors.

Although in several respects, upon its initial publication, *Tom Sawyer* appeared to be relatively successful, it did not produce any of the success for Twain he had expected it would. It actually sold in quantities far above that of many books at the time, and today, but the author chose to compare its success with his first major book, *Innocents Abroad*. That work, published in 1869, displayed unusual success in terms of copies sold and money earned for its time. Although *Tom Sawyer* sold, in its initial sales, one copy only compared to three for the earlier book, its popularity did not decline and grew steadily through the years. Before the author died, it had surpassed the sales of all his other titles.

As time went on and Twain grew aware of the increasing attention given *Tom Sawyer*, he reflected on the work as a "hymn" to childhood. This is an abstract description of the book and fits only its popular appeal. It does not begin to explain why the book continues to appeal to a wider audience that reaches into scholarship. Such a view misses its finest points. The secret of its appeal, if such can be isolated at all, is difficult to define. There are many books that utilize finer plots and many of those contain a higher grade of writing. Yet, few are the readers who are ever disappointed in *Tom Sawyer* and are apt to forget the story once they have read it.

This stimulates a demand to know more about such books and their background, no matter how difficult the problems which must be overcome. Those problems are particularly difficult regarding *Tom Sawyer*. It has a deceptively simple appearance, being a book which while centered in a particular place and time, also possesses universal appeal. It is made even more difficult by its author's complex, divided personality. Twain's methods and accomplishments are a continuing challenge to scholars. There is little wonder that such a book has produced many conflicting and mistaken opinions as to the reasons for its success and the history of its creation. The latter is made still more perplexing by the scarcity of reliable information. Whatever can be discovered in regard to the background of *Tom Sawyer*, though limited, adds to the knowledge of its author's life.

It is not uncommon for a work of fiction to have a strong relation to the life of its author. In some, the relationship appears to be more important than it is in others. So it appears to be in regard to *Tom Sawyer*, which does of course have definite autobiographical features. These features, however, often given too much attention in opinions about *Tom Sawyer*, are in truth mainly a frame and viewed best as only secondary in importance to the fiction that has been constructed upon them.

Most of the author's autobiographical contributions have been disguised heavily through the process of art, embellished with humor, seasoned with burlesque treatment, and bonded to the appealing adventures of the tale so cleverly that the facts are often inseparable from the fiction. Yet, in spite of the imbalance of fact and fiction contained in the work itself, its autobiographical nature has its own importance and to a degree was a part of the reasons for which it was written.

Twain worked on *Tom Sawyer* during those important years of his life and career when he was striving to establish himself as an author, bent intently on receiving recognition as such, but also on enjoying the benefits that might accompany such recognition. Because of this, the writing of this novel encompassed many of the problems Twain had as an author and is significant to any understanding of the author and his total work. The reasons the author wrote this novel, and they are several and mixed, therefore are basic to a thorough assessment of him.

The background begins with Twain's father. It was possibly the failures of his father, the poverty of his family, these combined with other reasons buried in his past, but the desire to be wealthy and respected was a central influence in almost every decision that Twain made regarding his future. He desired to be recognized as an important individual, accepted by his peers, and respected for his opinions — opinions he would frequently divulge only under the wrappings of his keen humor. Associated with this need for acceptance, and never secondary to it, was an aspiration to command enough riches to meet his extended ambitions. Ambitions as such are not unusual, but their complete fulfillment remains rare. Twain's decision, early in 1868, as his career was at a vital turning point, to write *Innocents Abroad* for a subscription publisher was a fortunate one toward the fulfillment of his hopes. The American Publishing Company associated him with a firm that was, by many accounts, the leader in the subscription book selling field.

The more common method of selling books, then and now, is to offer the merchandise for sale in bookstores and related establishments. Subscription book publishers devised an opposite method to distribute the bulk of their production. They hired and sent out an army of salespeople across the country, into every city and hamlet, penetrating into the farms and wilderness, armed with a sales manual featuring sample chapters and illustrations the published item would contain. The writing of customers' orders, at the onset, preceded the final printing and binding of the volume being sold. The ambitions of the salespeople, the selection of interesting samples from the text, and the numerous promised illustrations shown to potential customers were all important to the final success of a work. Through this combination of sales efforts such publishers managed to sell large quantities of books to persons and in places that bookstores never reached. Selling became a contest between the needs of the customer and the endurance of the salesperson working on a commission basis.

Many of the works sold by subscription were comparatively expensive since they were physically large in most cases, often issued as two volumes through the use of heavy paper, wide margins, and an abundance of illustrations. The books were also made even more expensive and appealing when provided a look of importance due to the use of highly decorative bindings, ranging from cloth to fine leathers. In spite of their price, the methods used sold vast numbers of copies, even of those whose contents were of a definitely inferior nature. The popular nature of a subject for a subscription publication was normally more important than the selection of an author, the author's ability secondary to that of their fame.

Twain was an unusual addition to the subscription book field — a decision made only after a vehement dispute among the directors of the American Publishing Company, but a wise decision which enriched the firm even more than it did the author. Seldom before or after Twain can there be found examples that defy outright the common principles followed by the subscription book selling method. Unlike the typical author, Twain was a humorist. He wrote more fiction than fact and he was superbly talented with the use of language — his choice of words, his style and variety of subject matter adding to his uniqueness. His initial success as a subscription book author probably surprised most everyone in the business except Elisha Bliss, the shrewd executive who first realized Twain's potential. It might be that Twain would not have had his initial success had he taken the course of most authors and published his work in the common manner (as he did on a limited scale with his first small volume which failed), even though his talents would seem to insure he might eventually become an author of note whatever the method of publication followed.

Mark Twain's first subscription book, *Innocents Abroad*, proved a double success, bringing both wealth and the attention of influential people (such as Howells). Impressed by this, he became devoted to the method and stuck with it the greater part of his active career. When his first work sold 67,000 copies during its first year, large by the standards of the time, that success caused him to overlook the many problems that followed with his publishers. Hoping to parlay his good fortune, he allowed himself to become heavily involved in the business details of publishing as well as the writing of books. While he had all of the necessary talent for the latter, he had little for the former. His relationship with Elisha Bliss went through many stages of ups and downs, frequently disturbing to his creative undertakings. In spite of these drawbacks, the subscription book selling method brought attention and good fortune in quantities that he might not otherwise have realized. That this all had its effect, both good and bad, upon the creation and popularity of *Tom Sawyer* is worth considering.

Two years after *Innocents Abroad* had established Twain as a popular author, it also allowed his marriage into a family of wealth to become a sudden reality. His success with that book increased the demand for his occasional sketches and his popular lectures many times over the previous demand. It allowed his next move, which was to put aside journalism as a profession and concentrate on writing books.

With his next book, *Roughing It*, his creative labors underwent a struggle in many ways. He worked persistently on the book in spite of the strain of a variety of outside and domestic interferences — most similar to those that were to appear again and again for the author. The subscription method again provided a measure of financial success. Yet, artistically considered, regardless of the fact that in a few places it contains examples of his finest work, *Roughing It* is an uneven book and needs to be judged with certain reservations. What success it brought provided Twain continuing hope for his prospects as an author and aided him in moving his family to Hartford, Connecticut, near the center of American culture for that time. Next, he made the inevitable trip to England and there received the accolades of many. Accompanying this fame was an increasing pressure to write still other popular and successful books, a necessity which furnished no easy retreat as it grew more and more important to his future.

*Innocents Abroad* had developed out of an actual tour Twain made to the Holy Lands, while *Roughing It* drew heavily from his experience in the West, yet both used ample amounts of fiction woven into their factual content. As it had from the very start of his career as a writer, fiction intrigued the author. Entire pieces of his early journalism and many of his early sketches not only have a portion of fiction woven into their factual content, but some are almost entirely woven out of fiction. When it seemed that the next logical progression in writing would require a further step back in time, the author conceived the idea that he might treat certain parts of his family's background in Missouri, along with incidents from his own childhood as a long work of fiction. In this, he decided, he might use some of the sketches and lecture material he had been working on during his first voyage to England, and earlier material that he had experimented with. The challenge to deal with this more sensitive part of his life apparently had much to do with his decision to treat the material more completely as fiction.

He wanted this to be another large book intended for subscription publication and directed at his wide adult audience which now included a readership in Europe that he wished to cultivate. Although his goal this time was a novel, his past writing experience tended to lead him into construction along the lines of interconnecting sketches, basically held together by a general theme, as his other successful books were constructed. Still, he was aware that this work would need a stronger and a more involved plot if it was to stand as a work of fiction. As he made his initial attempt to put together a manuscript, striving to write his particular type of humor, blending exaggeration and burlesque with a serious moral undercurrent, he began to feel the burden of inventing enough plotting material to sustain the length of the work he was aiming at.

Persistent from his earliest years and believing that he was a writer to challenge his contemporary authors, although he was disappointed at his initial efforts, he was not about to give in to despair and fail. It was at this point that he began his lengthy discussions with Charles Dudley Warner. At first his hope was that Warner might be able to furnish him some key to plotting that he could then use to organize the efforts he had embarked upon. Warner was probably of more aid as a soundingboard than as a teacher, but the experience of their discussion led Twain to a decision that the two men might coauthor a novel. This produced *The Gilded Age*. More than anything else it may have added to his stature, the novel done with Warner — each author following leads the other suggested — was of untold aid in providing the benefits of knowledge and confidence for the laboring with a long work of fiction that Twain had lacked up until then. With its completion, the author's dubious attitude toward writing a novel diminished.

Twain seemed to immensely enjoy the work he put into *The Gilded Age* and undertook promotion of it with great enthusiasm. The subscription publication of this awkwardly constructed satire on the popular novel and the politics of its time helped to increase its sales, profits, and popularity with the readers of its day. It sold in surprising numbers for a large work of fiction written by two authors not noted as novelists. Again, while it was a work primarily of fiction, much of it was composed out of actual incidents popularized in the newspapers, as well as slices out of the authors' lives.

Although drawing upon some of the material he had been struggling with during the previous year in his attempts to create a work of fiction, especially for the opening section, Twain did not share any of the Hannibal material with Warner on their project. This he reserved, preserving it for the time he made his next solo attempt. It would be used to furnish most of the first half of *Tom Sawyer*.

He had begun *Tom Sawyer* as a work intended for an adult audience, a work of *serious* humor, and when he went back to it his goal had not changed. It was begun and it was written as a book for adult readers. Whether he was fully aware of it, or not, it was a book that was important to his career as no other book he ever wrote.

# 7. An Acceptable Past

When Mark Twain married Olivia Langdon in 1870, a significant change came to his life. Although he had accomplished much by then for an individual of his means, that ceremony produced an awareness, as nothing else did, that he had one serious flaw, a past that was unassuring and shabby compared to the average individual belonging to that society with which he was determined to merge his life.

In the past he had said on many occasions that he despised the wealthy and successful people. Now, at intervals becoming more frequent, he indicated in various ways that he envied them, their power, their respect, and their inheritance. The past that most of them could look back upon, he had come to believe, was apparently different and more acceptable than the past that he had been associated with. Not only did he become aware of certain supposed deficiencies such as the poverty of his childhood, his frontier education, his wanderings as printer, pilot of river boats and Western journalist, but more recent experiences in New York and on his trip to the Holy Land caused him to grow sensitive that his past was littered with many things not usually convenient to boast about—unless they were recast in some inventive fashion.

The circumstances of Twain's past were depicted in sharp focus for him shortly before his engagement to Livy was announced, about a year before their wedding. In the customary manner of that time and society, Jervis Landon sought to secure an appraisal for his future son-in-law because Twain was a stranger in their midst, and in spite of a lately developing career as a journalist, the suitor had no established background to offer. There were a variety of rumors circulating about him. Likely, Langdon's son, Charley, having been a part of the small group of *Quaker City* tourists whom Twain had traveled with to the Holy Land and then wrote about, could have easily furnished other hints. Jervis Langdon, acting as any concerned father might, requested the budding author to list the names of friends who might supply information about the author's character.

Twain realized he faced a problem in fulfilling this request, for although he had made many friends, few of them could be termed refined persons compared to the Langdons and their friends. The dilemma was strengthened as he considered that most were rough mannered and fun-loving individuals like himself, and inclined to use any rare opportunity toward appraising a friend as a singular opportunity for ribaldry, more than they were likely to be helpful. Fearing Langdon would receive a number of invented and inflated revelations, in addition to the honest evaluations they could furnish, such that would result in serious damage to his chances for securing Oliva Langdon as his bride, Twain devised a list of names of "friends" for his prospective father-in-law made up of prominent persons, known casually to him or briefly by him — all of whom conveniently knew little about the journalist. It supplied him with hopes that they might automatically reply out of courtesy, furnishing answers sufficiently useful to ease him through the crisis.

The responses resulting from Langdon's letters of inquiry provided a near disaster. Virtually all the replies were negative. Looking back, years later, Twain described this whole affair with a touch of humor, but still aware of the biting appraisals: "They not only spoke in disapproval of me but they were quite unnecessarily and exaggeratedly enthusiastic about it."

Although during his conduct around the Langdon family in Elmira, New York, he had carefully exhibited manners beyond reproach, having cut down on his excesses of drinking, smoking, and swearing, added to a somewhat shaky return to a semblance of the Christian faith, his past offered very little to aid him in his quest for marriage to Livy. However, it was Twain's good fortune, which he seemed blessed with, that Jervis Langdon, aristocrat that he was, was also a gentleman with charitable instincts. Langdon, puzzled by the answers his letters had brought, asked the author, "What kind of people are these? Haven't you a friend in the world?" Twain unavoidably concluded that he apparently had none. Langdon then resolved the seeming hopelessness of the situation by telling the disheartened suitor, "I'll be your friend. Take the girl. I know you better than they do."

Although it proved a temporary victory, it was not a totally reassuring one. Twain knew from past experience that Livy's society, which he now sought to become a part of, was composed of few individuals as open-minded and as sympathetic as Jervis Langdon had shown himself. He knew that in order to survive in that society it was necessary to possess money, notable accomplishments, and the ability to establish a character, fabricated as it might need to be, that would overcome the rough, unpolished character that he was bringing with him. Mark Twain had one talent which set him apart and sustained him when all other things failed or were lacking. It was his exceptional ability to apply humor to most things, a trait that had brought him where he was, and which he accurately forecast would lead him to overcome his more obvious faults.

Always a sensitive and serious individual, Twain had learned early, partly by the example of his overburdened mother, to hide his deeper concerns under the trappings of humor. The use of humor was an art for him, one which he had grown so accomplished at handling that it was the primary tool he relied upon in most threatening situations. From the days of his teens, he had handled humor with a deft style that distinguished him from the others in his group wherever he went. It was a disarming humor, humor that seldom revealed the earnest, careful training he applied to improve and present it in a consistently calm, and casual manner. Only on rare occasions did it fail.

By the time of his marriage, Twain had refined his humor to the point that it had made him a professional success with increasing promise. As he reflected on his past, he could realize that his facility to use humor had helped him to surmount various obstacles which roughened his path, from a birth in a simple frontier society, through a poverty blighted childhood, and through several adventuresome occupations to the point at which he stood when he repeated the vows of marriage with Livy. He was surely well aware of the opportunity he had been presented, much the result of his own efforts, to become an accepted part of the prosperous, cultured society of the Eastern United States. He knew instinctively and without doubt that he could readily rely upon his exceptional ability, his talent for the creation of humor, to sustain his victory and to make any future improvements in his status.

From the moment of his wedding on, he knew he would need to depend upon the seeming magic his humor could perform to recreate his past in the form of a satire that would enable him to be, if not illustrious, at least acceptable in Livy's society. His apparent lack of any notable, glittering events that could impress the cultured East and its various pundits might be atoned for by using the basic truths, building upon them through the application of plain, folksy humor, satire, and the occasional anecdote until a sweetened disguise was created that would render the unillustrious facts appealing. It was a method he had been working to perfect from the days of his first efforts as "assistant editor" for his brother's Hannibal *Journal*, one he had honed carefully until he became a full-fledged journalist, and finally the author of a dynamic volume of satire that had brought him praise from some of the most highly rated authors of the society that he was bent upon entering.

The practice of fabricating his past, intentionally or not, had become almost a habitual routine for him by 1870. Using his own experiences as a frame upon which to weave his best writing, bending them, distorting them, and adding selective elements, some accurate, some revised, and many pure imagination, was the method he used with extraordinary success to fashion *Innocents Abroad*. In that book, while poking fun at himself, and at his fellow pilgrims, he somehow always seemed to come out, or appear at the end, as a hero. It was a method that worked also in his profitable lectures. Fabricated as the tales he wove about himself were, made to suit the need of his art, those reading his writings or hearing him at a lecture were immediately inclined to accept his telling of the stories as versions of reality.

It never appeared so much a decision to avoid truth as it was the direction in which his writing had developed, and in a somewhat similar fashion it brought him to believe that if he was to present his past as being acceptable to Livy's society, his surest opportunity for success would be realized by subjecting all of it to humor and satire. In regard to revelations of his personal life, from the beginning to the end, it was a practice that he would seldom ever abandon thereafter, even after a number of trials brought him tragic moments and difficult financial problems. Even after he had gained the respect of many, he preferred to use humor in his contact with the general public, although he could handle interviews with the deftness of any of his contemporaries. He also chose to suppress with humor the moralist nature that was natural for him, not because he was thoroughly serious, but because he was a sensitive person.

That part of his past which was to furnish the basis for *The Adventures of Tom Sawyer* was among the most sensitive. The bare-bone facts contained little that could ever be gloated over. From his earliest years he was raised almost as if fatherless — as he actually was after age 12. The family's poverty had always been a condition of their existence, and became critical when his father died. Although he had excellent moral training and the benefit of Christian teachings, he had been a rebel at heart from his earliest years, playing hooky from school and engaging in a wide range of youthful pranks. His formal education ended suddenly as a primary student shortly after his father's death. The society that he mingled with, then and for a long time after, was not one that was sympathetic to a sensitive mind. There had been more than a normal share of dreadful days and nights, and many of these he could not escape from; they lingered clearly in his memory for many years, even as they frequently troubled his sleep during his youth. Fortunately, there were also enough good days which, if only privately, he could look back upon — certain parts of his childhood that seemed an eternal summer — to sustain him as he grew to manhood. But, the failings of his father, the constant struggles of his mother to survive her widowhood with her children and her husband's debts, the lack of a thorough education, and the complete absence of any financial security were not subjects Twain talked about — unless they were made light of with the use of humor.

Although the actual success of turning this material into the adventures of "Tom Sawyer" remained some two years in the future, it is clear that he was abnormally sensitive to various experiences of his childhood a few days following his marriage of February 4, 1870, as he sat down on a Sunday afternoon to write a reply to a letter he had received from Will Bowen. As earlier writings reveal, he had always been mindful of certain aspects of his Hannibal days, for references creep into various phases of his work, in several sketches, in letters, and minutely — but certainly — in *Innocents Abroad*. Yet, in the reply he wrote to Bowen, there is indisputable evidence of a special awareness of his childhood days, of how particularly sensitive he was even when twenty or more years separated him from them.

Jervis Langdon may have been allowed an impression that Twain had no real friends, yet the letter to Bowen had clearly addressed him as "My First, & Oldest & Dearest Friend." Triggered by Bowen's letter, Twain wrote back, "The fountains of my great deep are broken up & I have rained reminiscences for four & twenty hours." Then following with a brief, trite, poetic description of his nostalgia, Twain listed in one long, rambling sentence some 16 distinctive instances recalled from his Hannibal childhood days that he had apparently shared with Bowen,

*Four women in Twain's life. Top left is Laura Hawkins, his "first sweetheart" and the model for Becky Thatcher. Top right is Olivia Langdon, whom he married. There exists an interesting comparison between the bottom illustrations, that (right) of Jane Clemens, the author's mother, and the illustration of Aunt Polly (left) from the American first edition. This last was not drawn by True Williams (see his on page 27) but duplicates an illustration of the character Ruth Partington in B.P. Shillaber's 1854* Life and Sayings of Mrs. Partington, *the stories about her nephew Ike having influenced Twain's creation of Tom Sawyer.*

until the mentioning of a seventeenth, a more personal recollection that he notes shocks him out of his reminiscing and brings his thoughts back to the present — the mention of his "sweetheart," Laura Hawkins.

Nearly half of the items Twain remembered bear a close relation to things that are later found as a part of the *Tom Sawyer* novel: the remainder also, but only more remotely. One recalls Jimmy Finn the "town drunkard" who slept in a vat, another refers to the playing of Robin Hood games dressed only in shirt-tails and using wood laths for swords "in the woods on Holliday's Hill." One refers to a day when the town thought Sam Clemens had drowned. Others recall school experiences and those of Sunday school. The final item, in which Twain notes, "since Laura Hawkins was my sweetheart — —" and breaks off, says little directly, but is a guarded reference to the rich material which was to be fashioned later into Tom's relationship to Becky Thatcher in the well-known story.

Upon this mention of Laura Hawkins, Twain ends the listing of his memories as if a sensitive nerve had been touched, continuing toward the conclusion of his letter with a self-conscious description of his good fortune resulting from his marriage to Livy. He describes her as "the very most perfect gem of womankind that ever I saw in my life." He is aware of the extensive change she is making in his life style. As a result, he told Bowen, "Wherefore without effort, or struggle, or spoken exorcism, all the old vices & shameful habits that have possessed me these many years are falling away, one by one, & departing into the darkness."

It was the way he would have wished it, but he knew very well that they would not disappear entirely even with extra efforts. A person of some 34 years cannot cast off with ease past habits that have taken deep root in the composure of his or her character — and Twain carried with him an accumulation varied enough to have full knowledge of the truth. His past was to effectively stay with him in some form, even if only in the form of memories, no matter how carefully he directed his future course of action; but, what could not be discarded, rightly handled, could be disguised. It was a method that worked well for him in most cases, making up for deficiencies, literally turning lead into gold — failing only rarely, as it did sometimes with persons like the wife of Thomas Bailey Aldrich, even occasionally with Livy, most of the failings coming when Twain bore down too hard.

Within a few months following his wedding, perhaps even with days, he made a recorded attempt in the direction of putting his past to humor, an attempt which did not succeed. The evidence is in a manuscript which Albert Bigelow Paine, first curator of Mark Twain's papers, named "Boy's Manuscript." This writing, which remained unpublished for many years (until critic and author Bernard DeVoto, then the succeeding curator, brought it to light), is important, even as a failure, in the use of humor to remake an image of the past because of its direct relationship to the more successful *Tom Sawyer*.

# 8. A Misguided Sketch

Perhaps there is only one reason to read the "Boy's Manuscript," which is to see how Mark Twain treated his unusual interest in his Hannibal childhood long before he began *Tom Sawyer*. The immature way he did so is clearly demonstrated in comparing this sketch and the published novel. There is an obvious self-consciousness, a hint of insecurity in the earlier manuscript, that produce an awkwardness almost totally absent from the novel, characterized by its sharper focus, its freedom from sentiment even in the dark moments of the adventures. These differences appear stark, even as the reader realizes that there is a direct link between much in the shorter item and the longer, later work.

Bernard DeVoto first announced the "Boy's Manuscript" was a direct predecessor to the novel. In it he saw early evidence of Twain struggling with the material of his Hannibal past, striving to transpose it into a formal narrative device. DeVoto considered it a crude performance, but as a step toward the novel it was significant. Although there were parts of these childhood experiences incorporated in several sketches and particularly in some of the author's early letters, no earlier attempt had ever been undertaken to write anything as lengthy using the material as the prime theme.

In one of his letters to Bowen in 1868, Twain exclaimed how he had used an incident from their school days involving the sale of a louse (similar to the event later used in the "Boy's Manuscript," but changed to the tick incident in *Tom Sawyer*) to provoke a rousing laugh from a group of members of the Congress to whom the author had spoken. To Bowen, he noted: "It was a gorgeous old reminiscence. I just expect I shall publish it yet someday." This prediction proved accurate, yet there is no evidence in 1868 that he planned to use it except as an anecdote, or at the most as the center for a short sketch.

It indicates, as did the 1870 letter to Bowen shortly after Twain's marriage, an active awareness of the Hannibal years, particular parts of a past that could not be wholly repressed, a mixture of things both good and bad. While his marriage was a means whereby he could move beyond that past, reaching new and important heights of experience, he realized that this could only take place as he compensated for that past. This awareness of what he believed necessary to enjoy his newly found status played a large part in the formation of the burlesque treatment of the events surrounding "Billy Rogers."

It is not known exactly when the "Boy's Manuscript" was written, but Paine's notation on the manuscript, "Probably written about 1870," appears to be accurate. DeVoto cites evidence that the Paine date is probably correct based on not only the type of ink used, the type of paper used, but also is indicated by the author's handwriting. A more precise date for the writing of the manuscript within that year is open to speculation, the author not having mentioned it anywhere — but several things suggest that it was written shortly after the date of his wedding, probably in a period that would range from a few days to several months. If a prime reason for it was a desire for recasting his past in a humorous vein, one aimed in part at improving the chances of making it more acceptable, brought about by the intensified focus on the identity problem he faced in his adopted society, the choice of a date near his marriage would seem to be reasonable.

If, as some critics suggest, one of the chief themes of the "Boy's Manuscript" is burlesquing the traditions of courtship and marriage prevailing then, it can be reasonably expected that Twain composed it shortly after he himself had successfully picked his path through those same events. Certainly, what he was doing and the change that was taking place in his life weighed heavily on the author's thoughts — and well might have affected the directions such writing took.

It should also be noted that Twain had signed the contract resulting in *Roughing It* on July 15, 1870, and thus he was soon working on its manuscript, using whatever time could be made available as he pushed aside his editorial and business duties with the Buffalo *Express*. If the correct year has been assigned to the "Boy's Manuscript," then it appears that any opportunities and inspirations needed for its composition would have been more readily available during the first half of that year. An exact date, however, is relatively unimportant except as it reflects on the anticipation of the later novel.

Nothing about the extended sketch suggests that it might have been written as the first step toward creation of a novel. It is longer by far than the average performance of this type by the author but comes to a logical ending, suggesting that those pages of the existing manuscript are likely to be all that were ever intended. While the material used here and to a lesser degree the manner in which it is presented all point definitely to its being his initial start toward the writing of *Tom Sawyer*, there is nothing in this particular piece or in Twain's methods to this time to suggest that the writing of a novel was among the author's plans. All of his early books were basically constructed from the accumulation of sketches, these being the normal creative form governing his work. Sketches were the form upon which his writing skills had been developed — in his journalism he had found them the most suitable form for his purpose, and when he began to think in terms of books he saw them as the units needed to construct the longer manuscripts.

DeVoto has also declared that the "Boy's Manuscript" appears to be Mark Twain's first attempt at straight fiction (discounting the fictional quality of many of his sketches), as well as the first full scale use of the Hannibal material. While such may be the case, the evidence is minimal to suggest that a primary objective for the writing of this manuscript was for publication. A more elusive reason, perhaps a personal one, is more evident as its structure is examined. If Twain was thinking in terms of putting his nondescript past into a humorous form to temper its effect, perhaps he automatically reached for his pen from force of habit as a writer and began to toy with thoughts of turning it into fiction. He had, by then, already demonstrated that he frequently would rehearse parts of his work far in advance of using them in a finished work. His childhood romance with Laura Hawkins still smoldered to such a degree in his recollections, that even to a writer of his then limited experience, he realized that to write about it he needed to muffle the sentiment it created and which he carried with him, reforming beneath the weight of heavy-handed humor whatever could be used in any fashion. He knew that it could not be a part of the past that he was reconstructing for use in his new social setting unless it was properly subdued. If the writing of the "Boy's Manuscript" was purely an attempt to subdue his personal feelings in this manner, it may be that the preservation of this sketch was purely an accident, if not an unconscious act. Whatever the actual reason for the origin of this item, awkward as a sketch, interesting as evidence of the author's mind and methods, a number of factors seem to merge in it, and the attempt to write fiction, much less a novel, seems only one limited possibility.

Whatever the author's reasons for writing it, aside from its serving to formulate some of the material that would later be dealt with in *Tom Sawyer*, he showed wisdom in casting it aside as unworthy of his abilities. In contrast to *Tom Sawyer*, it presents a self-centered, childish hero who is worthy of none of the sympathy that Tom generates. Its tone irritates the reader more than it interests, in part because of the method of narration, using the first person in diary form. Whether Billy Rogers is boasting or whining, his plight remains largely one of his own making. He seems to deserve worse than what he gets.

The psychological implications seem even more fertile as they become elusive. While drawing basically upon experiences from his personal past, Twain subjects his material to a barrage of elements of burlesque, making use of contrasts that are both obvious and overburdened in every sense. The more subtle burlesque of *Tom Sawyer* and other successful writings from the author's pen is missing in this manuscript in every paragraph, and in its stead the reader is continually rapped with jokes that are no more potent than an inflated bladder. Burlesque for the sake of burlesque became the trap he stumbled into in this sketch, ridiculing the ridiculous with no resort to subtlety. Its survival must be laid to sentimental reasons.

The "Boy's Manuscript" is itself unimportant and needs to be studied in some detail only for its provision of whatever background it can furnish for the creation of *Tom Sawyer*. Pages one and two of the manuscript are missing, for whatever reason, and it begins on the third page with "me that put the apple there." This is "Monday's" entry to the diary, describing the agonies Billy Rogers is going through as a result of putting an apple on the doorstep of "Sweet Amy" on Sunday. Amy is apparently a petite neighbor girl near Billy's age, about eight, wearing blue ribbons and white frocks, who has just moved into Billy's environment. Although this apple incident did not become a part of *Tom Sawyer*, its details resemble the first awareness of Tom for Becky Thatcher. The placing of the apple for Amy to find can be seen as a pure, simple, typical childlike action and reaction, without connotations or symbolism, although the possibility that the author chose the apple as symbolic cannot be totally dismissed.

"Tuesday" has Billy reporting that he played hooky and hung around watching the windows of Amy's house for a glimpse of the girl, but is rewarded only by a glimpse of the chambermaid. This is, as is quickly recognized, material that was remolded into *Tom Sawyer*. Next, there follows some revelations of a torchlight procession. The display of "showing off" by Billy Rogers is typical of Tom Sawyer's showing off; but Billy, unlike Tom, pays out his marbles, fishhooks, and extracted teeth to get acquainted with Amy's brother, "Tom," who is all but written off after his initial appearance. Also brief is the mention of meeting Amy's father and mother, of whom Billy says, "They seem like kings and queens to me." This material was to be later amplified with slight changes in *Tom Sawyer* as Tom reflects upon Becky's father, Judge Thatcher. Observing, finally, that Amy's brother "can hug and kiss her whenever he wants to," the writer closes this section with the cryptic, "I wish I was her brother. But it can't be, I don't reckon!" Here Twain, while ostensibly depicting a child's innocence and confusion in matters of sexual knowledge, may also be teasing with a remote hint of youthful incestuous thoughts. In a few other instances in Twain's writings sexually suggestive themes stir slightly and muddily beneath the surface.

"Wednesday" the entry again records some Tom Sawyer-like behavior and includes a list of the contents of Billy's pants pockets, ranging from a "spool cannon" to a "door knob" and including "a picture of Adam and Eve without a rag." This day closes with thoughts of the effects of self-destruction, Billy noting, "I wish I was dead.... Then maybe she would be sorry," a creative seed that provides little indication of the expanded material that features the running-away-to-the-island episode and the self-witnessed funeral of *Tom Sawyer*. There the desire for feelings of sorrow come secondary, even as they become legitimate feelings. In his record for "Friday," Billy reveals the misinterpretation by his mother of his puppy love despondency as the advent of an illness, whereupon she, like "Aunt Polly" treating Tom, gives Billy abusive medicines and treatments meant for a cure.

The "Saturday Night" section begins, "This was a blessed day." Amy's aunt, Mrs. Johnson, visits the Rogers and brings Amy with her. Finally, Billy and Amy are brought face to face and a section of straight dialogue results. This has none of the polish of later *Tom Sawyer*'s dialogue, and the constant attempts at humor are mediocre, even though they are intended only as words out of the mouths of children. Here, the obvious posing or imposing of the author shows clearly in every line. The dialogue provides little of value for the sketch except as an introduction to the young pair's school days.

With no explanation, the diary skips to Thursday of the next week.

Billy reveals that he and Amy have been "playing together three days," adding "and to-day I asked her if she would be my little wife and she said she would," reflecting upon the more appealing "engagement" scene of Tom and Becky. This event ends with the appearance of "Jim Riley and Bob Sawyer" who have overheard Billy and Amy, and leads to Billy "licking" Jim Riley, Bob Sawyer licking Billy, and "Jo Bryant" licking Sawyer, whereupon the teacher licks them all. Here Mark Twain's initial use of "Sawyer" as a surname catches the reader's eye, but only briefly for Bob Sawyer makes no other appearance. Why it is adopted for the later hero has been the subject of debate, but never resolved. Here, it can be supposed, it carries no extra implications, although within a few years the author transforms Billy Rogers to Tom Sawyer. Yet, there is always the feeling that Twain selected the names of his characters with purpose, if only at times for the tonal effects, though he has also been shown to be careless with the names of his characters from manuscript to manuscript, and even within a manuscript, as he was in writing *Tom Sawyer*. The question as to how "Billy Rogers" evolved into "Tom Sawyer" is a reasonable one to ask, but there seems to be no reasonable answer.

After Amy has gone away crying, the entry for "Friday" turns to gloom, Billy writing, "The world is all dark to me." (How trivial this appears compared to the darkness of the cave that Tom and Becky later face.) Billy Rogers is entangled in a web of despair, but he loves it. "Saturday" reveals a return to ideas of self-destruction again, but each method of suicide is cancelled out by humorous circumstances, such as the final in which a bottle of castor oil is drunk and by the next morning Billy remarks he "had lost all interest in things...." (Similar adventures into slight grossness, or "various obscenities" as they were designated by the author, had been a part of *Tom Sawyer* until they were removed upon the advice of Howells.) Fate, however, repeats itself and the two "lovers" are reunited again at the sickbed. (Here, while we are reminded of similarities to Twain's courtship experiences, the similarities may be just as easily dismissed.) This entry closes with Billy, again exhibiting his typical Tom Sawyer-like personality, declaring he is going to become a pirate. Appearing almost to be a line out of the later book, Billy relates that he dreams of strolling into his Sunday School with "long black hair, and my slouch hat with a plume in it, and my long sword and high boots and a splendid belt and red satin doublet and breeches, and my black flag with scull and cross-bones on it, and all the children will say, 'Look—look—that's Rogers the pirate!'" It can not be said better than DeVoto did, "We are well within Tom Sawyer's mind...."

Skipping, again with no explanation, to "Tuesday," Billy Rogers is present, dreaming, looking out of the schoolhouse window, wishing to be "free and far away." This day also reveals a relationship to *Tom Sawyer*, utilizing here the favored recollection of the author about a game played in school using a purchased louse. Here threads tightly connect fact to fiction, for Billy Rogers attributes ownership of the louse to his "chum, Bill Bowen," an obvious reference to the real Will Bowen and what the author had consistently referred to as an actual event from his Hannibal past, again so stated here in an added note initialed "M.T." (This notation furnishes the only evidence, if any, that the author may have had some thoughts of publication.)

Having apparently lost all patience with a day by day accounting, the author skips, unaccountably again, in the next two segments to "Tuesday Week" and "Tuesday Fortnight." The first Tuesday, other than for mention of a "wooden sword" and a children's game of "army," is significant for the appearance of "Wart Hopkins." Wart Hopkin's chief importance is that he appears to be an early model of "Huckleberry Finn." Billy Rogers, overtaken by Wart Hopkins, explains, "He's been out to the crossroads burying a bean that he'd bloodied with a wart to make them go away...." Unlike the later, likeable Huck, Billy describes Wart as "always mean." Wart Hopkins is only a shadow of Huckleberry Finn, the outline and no more.

Wart Hopkins is also "suffering" because he "loved Susan Hawkins and she was gone to the country too." Since it can be demonstrated that Huckleberry Finn is the alter ego of Tom Sawyer, as both characters exhibit to a degree reverse sides of their creator, the question needs to be asked here: Can Wart Hopkins be an alter ego of Billy Rogers, both of these originating to a degree from their divided creator? It may be, for the author describes Wart Hopkins through a series of descriptions of activities which mirror activities of Billy Rogers, strengthening whatever implications there are here. Also, the use of the name "Hawkins" reveals the author shuffling names again, for Amy (an "Amy Lawrence" later becoming the earlier sweetheart of Tom Sawyer) is a reflection of Becky Thatcher, while Becky Thatcher has ties running to Susan Hawkins (Laura Hawkins, the author's childhood sweetheart, having the same surname). The importance of Laura Hawkins to the origin of this manuscript, and then to *Tom Sawyer*, seems to be more than the records will reveal. In a sense, every little girl character in material using the Hannibal experiences of the author is to some extent a reflection of the real Laura Hawkins, as Tom Sawyer and Billy Rogers are of young Sam Clemens, almost two decades before he slipped into his Mark Twain disguise.

The depiction of the romance in the "Boy's Manuscript," compared on various points to the treatment rendered to similar material in *Tom Sawyer*, exhibits clear differences. In this sketch the romance is central and is dwelt upon at length, the verbalizations consistently more silly than melodramatic. By "Tuesday Fortnight" the romance flags and becomes repetitive, losing whatever initial vitality it may have had. Billy Rogers, clearly showing masochistic tendencies, gives indications of enjoying the pain it brings him. He has completed the circle and laments, "I'll never love another girl again. There's no dependence in them.... I can't write her name, for the tears will come. But she has treated me shamefully." Still, at another time he wants "to rush there and grab her in my arms and be friends again." Whether this indecisiveness is strictly a literary pose, or whether it has resulted from some of the recollections of the author that rise from the "fountains of my great depth," as he once remarked to Bowen, is an entreating question.

The implications continue with the ending of the sketch, stated as "Saturday." That day Billy Rogers falls in love with another girl, in spite of his vow. "I shall die if I cannot get her," he continues his pose. Then, he reports that he had blindly mistaken her dropping the leaf of a flower for "a tall young man" as intended for himself, though never outrightly admitting his error. While, on the basis of the evidence given, Billy can at best be assigned an age of eight, his new idol is nineteen. He states: "Her name's Laura Miller.... I never, never will part with *this* one! NEVER." So, teasing and enigmatic, the play with names continues, "Laura Miller" not only echoing again Laura Hawkins (placed in her teen years), but also an older girl by the name of Mary Miller whom Mark Twain once "fell in love" with according to a paragraph from his *Autobiography*.

How close to autobiography is this sketch? The "louse" incident is confirmed by the author. The closing "diary" entry shows a basis for reality according to autobiographical items. Certainly, parts of the character and behavior of Billy Rogers reflect some of the known character and behavior of the creator in his Hannibal days. On whether this manuscript is a disguised reconstruction of actual events, whether it was begun as a rehearsal of an acceptable recasting of that past redressed in humor, whether as it expanded the raw material grew more fictional, whether the author eventually began to consider the consequences of publication (as most authors do regarding that which they write), and whether the final reality of it was too painful to permit further thoughts of publication, no answer can be given. But the importance that this manuscript has to the *Tom Sawyer* novel into which it finally evolved, reflects the importance which the author himself may have placed on it.

While observing that *Tom Sawyer* began with this sketch, it must also be observed that it began here only in a relative sense. Some of the novel's material is here, but not much of its quality. The "Boy's Manuscript," however interesting as a preliminary sketch, lacks all of Tom Sawyer's explicit virtures, the novel's control of melodramatic sentiments and the balance of the real world against the child's world.

Abandoned by the author in favor of *Tom Sawyer* and overlooked by Albert Bigelow Paine, the text of "Boy's Manuscript" was published first as a part of Bernard DeVoto's introduction to the Limited Editions Club edition of *Tom Sawyer* (1939) and later in his *Mark Twain at Work* (1942). It has now been included, along with a "Genetic Text" version illustrating the few minor changes Mark Twain applied to his manuscript, in Volume 4 of *The Works of Mark Twain* (Iowa Center for Textual Studies/University of California Press, 1980). As background material to the writing of *Tom Sawyer*, this sketch reveals several things — but of major importance is the relationship of the Hannibal recollections to his marriage and career at the time the author composed these pages.

# 9. The Story of a Bad Boy

The background elements in Mark Twain's career to 1874 that led to the writing of *Tom Sawyer* are multiple and intermixed. They are all important, if not equally important, and began to form early in his life. First and most prominent among all influences were the Hannibal experiences of his boyhood, without which there would never have been a *Tom Sawyer*. Somehow, this group of experiences and influences began to emerge in response to his felt need for the creating of an acceptable past, one he decided would be treated best through the use of humor.

During the period when he met and fell in love with Olivia Langdon, deciding to marry her and endeavoring to join the front ranks of an elite society dominant in the affairs of culture and commerce in the Eastern states, his need for creating an acceptable past gradually became a nucleus for all of the other forces operating in his life. Twain's advantages had been limited. He was without any advanced formal education and had lived on the edge of poverty almost to the time of his marriage. He was unsure in what manner the cultural leaders of that society might rank him. Already, by this stage, he was a most complex personality whose mind operated on several levels. Experience and self-training, plus a dash of luck and a touch of fate, had made him a journalist, a humorist, a lecturer, and beneath his roughened surface a moralist. He was an expert in the use of language and could skillfully string words together, twisting them at the right point to form a unique brand of humor and satire readily understood by a general audience. He had over the years developed an acquaintance with the classics above that of the average person, though beneath that of a trained scholar. He had seen life in most of its prominent facets and had traveled to a number of exotic places in the world. Somehow, he had a revelation, if not outright knowledge, that he had to put this all together if he were to succeed in his new status.

Although on the surface *Tom Sawyer* appears a simple, nostalgic tale of American boyhood, it is also a complex work reinforced by several levels, that gradually reveal themselves upon investigation. As a result of the several major forces operating in Twain's life, the novel was created with a nod to humor, an undercurrent of influence from the classics, and an attempt to make a moral statement. These disparate motives blend with the story, though the development of each may be isolated and examined separately to a degree.

The influence of humor developed very early in his life, a vital part of his Hannibal years. About the time of his childhood the popular humorous sketch was growing rapidly in prominence as a result of the increase in publishing for the ordinary citizen. Inevitably he would have

59

read this type of humor with enthusiasm. Although this humor includes varieties of several classifications, most of it might be termed merely "popular American mid-nineteenth century" humor. Circulated widely during Twain's formative years, it was featured in most of the inexpensive popular journals and as an item of usefulness in many of the small newspapers. Eventually some of it found its way into books. The genre included the story telling of the "Yankee" humorists, Seba Smith, creator of "Jack Downing"; Thomas Chandler Haliburton, creator of "Sam Slick"; James Russell Lowell, creator of "Hosea Biglow"; and their imitators and likes.

It also includes some frontier humor and Southwestern humor. There were authors collecting, rewriting, and creating varying shades of humor that can be fit into this category: William Trotter Porter, Augustus B. Longstreet, William T. Thompson, Johnson J. Hopper, George W. Harris, T.B. Thorpe, Henry T. Lewis, Joseph Glover Baldwin, and a host of other names, many now obscure if not by time then by the quality of the work. How much of this humor Twain was aware of is impossible to determine with accuracy, but he was surely aware of much of it, and certainly aware of most of its varieties.

Almost all of the examples of this type of humorous writing are given only limited attention today, principally by the students of early American literature. But, for a lengthy period, it was both a popular and a forceful literature, lingering yet today in some of the simpler environments in its simpler forms. Frequently, those whose tastes encompass more serious literature judge most of it to be trash, seldom finding any redeeming values in more than a limited portion. Yet, when compared to the traditional classics read by the educated, this type of literature was read by hundreds of thousands more in the horde of inexpensive publications in which it regularly appeared. It served the masses of readers in the middle years of the nineteenth century as comic books, paperbacks, and television do in the second half of the twentieth. Sometimes it was well written, but more frequently it was poorly done, its subject more of concern than its style. The vulgarity attached to it was not so much because of substance as taste.

Many schoolmasters and schoolmistresses — among those who considered their learning abused by this "low" type of humor — forbade the reading of it and at any given opportunity were ready to condemn it. Like a number of youngsters, young Sam Clemens, with his early and intensive interest in reading, inevitably discovered this readily available material and, given the circumstances of his surroundings and his character, found much pleasure in reading it side by side with his school books, the Bible, and those classics that were available to him.

Once when interviewed late in her life, Laura Hawkins provided a recollection of the young Sam Clemens which related how he came upon a Yankee "pack-pedlar" one day who was passing through Hannibal. This peddler had spread out his merchandise on the ground in the vicinity of the "town pump." She noted that "Sam became fascinated by a book with a bright yellow-cover, Judge Halliburton's 'Clockmaker,' giving the adventures of Sam Slick." Learning that the price the peddler asked seemed to be "a tarnation of a bargain," young Clemens borrowed a nickel, Laura related, given her by her father for candy, to which Sam then added some "stray pennies" from his close friends John Briggs, Gull Brady, and other boys present. Adding these resources to his own, he proceeded to do "some haggling" to further reduce the purchase price.

When the interviewer asked Laura if Mark Twain had liked the book, she replied, "Why, for weeks after that, every chance he got — even in church on one occasion! — he was reading that old book and laughing aloud."

The event recalled by Laura Hawkins probably happened even before he went to work in the local print shops, first as an apprentice working for one Hannibal newspaper, then later employed as an "assistant" to his older brother who entered the newspaper business in Hannibal, the author's age being in the neighborhood of 16. In these surroundings he would have had many more opportunities to read this type of humor, which appeared in many of the journals and newspapers exchanged regularly by such establishments. Not only did the print shops provide him with a ready source of such material, they also encouraged him to try his own hand at creating a similar type of humor at a very early age.

The importance of this type of humor to the formation and development of Mark Twain's writing is seen in the many surviving examples of his early published material. The items published in his brother's paper, when the brother had some occasion to be away and placed young Twain in charge, all show some influence of this humor. Already reaching out beyond Hannibal when he was only 17, items were submitted to Eastern publications. How many went and were accepted is not known, but two have been found that are traceable to efforts of the author. One of these is an item signed "S.L.C." and titled "The Dandy Frightening the Squatter." Containing a reference to Hannibal, it is likely from the hand of Mark Twain. This short humorous piece was published in Boston by *The Carpet-Bag* in its May 1, 1852, issue, a publication notable for its makeup of popular humorous material. The author had just begun to develop his interest in writing and this piece indicates that he took as his first model this stereotyped form of popular humor. Though he would later refine his presentations of such humor, the source of his acquaintance is obvious, and his interest was basic both to the style and content of much of his work.

Also, the importance of his acquaintance with the popular humor prevailing in his youth is shown in the texture of many of his letters and published items that he wrote when he left Hannibal to become a typesetter in various places, and during his several years as a Mississippi steamboat pilot. It appears to shape his writing with a heavy hand when, following his mining adventures in Nevada, he joined the staff of the Virginia City *Territorial Enterprise* as a reporter: there he was just as likely to conceive a "hoax" story as to report the straight facts of an event. His tendency to merge exaggeration with wit in his submitted items is frequently apparent in the surviving examples of his work there.

The influence of this type of popular humor continues to be an important factor during his San Francisco days, both as a newsman and when his "Jumping Frog of Calaveras County" story was published in the New York *Saturday Press* on November 18, 1865, making "Mark Twain" a nationally recognized name for the first time. The striking simularities of this story to the general context of the popular humorous literature that had appealed to him over the preceding years is clear evidence of his devotion to that type of work. However, he had recognized his own abilities and soon spoke of that famed story as "a villainous backwoods sketch."

Certainly, humor was one of his prime interests as can be seen from the outstanding success he had with it. Very early on in his career he learned to use it to hide some of his more serious, moralistic thinking. This serious side of his background, which he subdued at first, allowing it to dominate his writing only in his later years, was also an important factor from his earliest days in Hannibal. There, soon after he learned to read, he became acquainted with literature of a higher grade than mere humor. Many of the more generally acceptable works of classical status were obtainable, and even handy, within his orbit. The influence of his father and those books that, from all appearances, may be associated with John Clemens (he being one of the persons founding a library in early Hannibal) may have even predated young Sam's acquaintance with humor. The Bible, Shakespeare, Milton, and other readily accessible items were read at various times in the home, the school, and in his Sunday school classes. In all likelihood, Twain had many intensive encounters with some of the more available classics. Although this contact is not as readily seen in his youthful writing as is his reading of humor, it begins to appear while he is still yet a young man. As he went from his school days into employment in the print shops, his love of reading followed him and there is evidence that he sought out reading material wherever he went, drawn to it like a magnet. Never a formal scholar beyond his grade school years, Twain's selection of what he read was normally influenced as much by chance as it was by any determination to be selective.

At the close of a letter written during his eighteenth year, while working in New York during his first journey away from Hannibal, the author replied to his brother: "You ask where I spend my evenings. Where would you suppose, with a free printer's library containing more than 4,000 volumes within a quarter mile of me, and nobody at home to talk to?" Unlike some more deliberately calculated statements of the author, this one has an air of honesty. We see the young Mark Twain slowly moving towards writing the books that would bring him lasting fame by reading good books of all types, including the classics. While he did some sightseeing and attended theatrical performances on other occasions, the bulk of his free hours were probably given to the reading of many books.

After a brief return to Missouri, then some days spent in Iowa where he was again working in a print shop run by his older brother, Twain once more set out on his own, purportedly to undertake adventures surrounding the searching for riches in the Amazon country. In need of money to follow through on his dream, being vastly underpaid or unpaid by his brother, he went in 1856 to Cincinnati, then a center for publishing in the Midwest. Some letters he wrote on assignment to the Keokuk *Saturday Post* show that writing a burlesque form of humor was a prime interest at that time. Signed as the work of a country bumpkin, "Snodgrass," they illustrate the importance of this form of writing to the youth — but there are abundant hints in the evidence of his life by this point that he had already become well read in the more substantial forms of literature and learning.

In a later account of his days spent in Cincinnati, Twain wrote that he had met a Scotsman by the name of Macfarlane, a fellow boarder with whom he spent long hours discussing various serious works, including history, philosophy, science, the Bible, placing great emphasis on the dictionary. Although some features of the account might be discounted, the name "Macfarlane" appears to be a variant, if not a substitute, for one or more of others whose names he had forgotten. While various features of the discussions and their weighty subject matter may have been pursued less intensely than he later described, there undoubtedly remain portions of truth in this recollection.

By the time that Twain signed on as a student pilot, shortly becoming a regular member of crews operating steamboats between St. Louis and New Orleans, it is probable that he was constantly reading in a wide range of subjects. That job gave him many free hours and by this time much of his reading was of both classical works and certain of the currently popular authors, particularly including the writing of an author with an enormous popularity among general readers, Charles Dickens.

Although he was never to receive the benefits of a formal college education, Twain's several years spent up until the start of the Civil War working on the river provided him with some opportunities equivalent to or better than enrollment in college. He learned discipline from the training needed to become a pilot, experienced unusual opportunities to absorb the cultural life of two great cities and all that lay between them, and was amply exposed to all types of individuals, the higher, the lower, and the unique, and all of the variety of tests they made upon his character and intelligence. Twain made the claim later about every type of character he met in books that "I had known him before — met him on the river."

Life as a pilot on the Mississippi was a pronounced step in his maturity as a person and as an eventual author. Those experiences on the river set the main course of his career and resulted in his finest writings, but without the reading that he engaged in at the same time they might all have been wasted. There are indications that Twain's reading of Dickens had a definite influence on parts of his own work, a particular example being shown in the writing of the "Boy's Manuscript," and including *Tom Sawyer* but to a less relative degree. Franklin R. Rogers in the volume *Mark Twain's Burlesque Patterns* discusses the examples of this in depth. Much evidence is assembled by Rogers to demonstrate that Twain took Dickens as a prime model and source. Simularities between instances in *David Cooperfield* and the "Boy's Manuscript" are noted, suggesting strong evidence that the author may have intended a parody of Dickens' story in the writing of that sketch, or at least that the model was so much in mind that its shadow lingers in Twain's manuscript.

The degree to which Dickens played a part in the author's life was emphasized by a statement made in 1879, "You know I have always been a great admirer of Dickens, and his 'Tale of Two Cities.' I read it at least every two years. Dickens witnessed my first holding of hands with Livy when I took her to one of his lectures in New York."

Although the blending of Dickens' influence upon *Tom Sawyer* was handled in a more subtle fashion, it only helps in part to understand the direction the work took. More visible is the influence of another author and work: Cervantes' *Don Quixote* is responsible for other directions in which the novel developed. Just when Twain first read Cervantes' great work is not clear, but Olin Harris Moore, who wrote the initial essay on this relationship, "Mark Twain and Don Quixote," published in 1922, stated, "It is probable that Mark Twain had begun to read Cervantes as early as [the writing of] Innocents Abroad." Others believe with good reason, however, that he may have read it earlier, even while still in Hannibal. It is not improbable that he read it both as a boy and as an adult, certain elements of the humor appealing to the boy, with the adult able to profit more greatly from the implications of the satire.

Whatever the case, he certainly read it and the influence it had upon his own work is readily visible. Moore explains, "...there is a striking parallel between the plots of *Don Quixote*, on the one hand, and of *Tom Sawyer* and *Huckleberry Finn*, on the other." Moore cites instances, suggesting, "For the man Don Quixote Mark Twain substitutes the boy Tom Sawyer." Although Tom Sawyer is considered to be in essence modeled upon Mark Twain himself as a boy, and perhaps in some instances on certain boyhood pals, certain characteristics of Don Quixote, Moore explains, were necessarily substituted to make Tom reflect Cervantes' hero. How much effect reading *Don Quixote* had upon the actual shaping of *Tom Sawyer* is an open question, but it was without doubt a strong influence. Moore points out, "The humor of Mark Twain, as well as of Cervantes, lies to a great extent in the contrast between imaginative and unimaginative characters." This concept began to develop in Twain at a very early age, whether because of a reading of Cervantes' work, or more likely as a result of his daily experiences with a variety of persons at an early age. However, a later reading of Cervantes could have helped to formulate the concept more vividly for the author of *Tom Sawyer*, coming when he first began thinking of the work in terms of a picaresque-type epic. It is more credible as a rule to say that Mark Twain only parodies *Don Quixote*. In a wider sense, parody became only one of the elements that seem to have left an impression upon the novel. In all, there is little question that much of Cervantes' work lay in the background during certain stages of the writing of *Tom Sawyer*, as it seems to have during the writing of others of his manuscripts.

Important to the writing of *Tom Sawyer* as the various influences of Dickens and Cervantes were, there were also other strong influences at work, some a part of classical tradition, others coming from more popular literature. Their influences are equally evident.

One kind of popular literature, frequently cited and often labeled as "bad boy literature," had a strong, direct effect on the early sketches that grew into the book. This class of writing appeared as a reaction to the "model boy" class of literature, one produced primarily for consumption in homes with firm religious standards, the schools, and for distribution in Sunday school classes. Model boy literature developed its original prominence following the publication in 1827 of the first of the many "Peter Parley" books by Samuel G. Goodrich. These were joined by the "little Rollo" stories of Jacob Abbott, first in 1835 and in many following stories. Their primary objective has been explained as an attempt "to spiritualize the mind," a feat as difficult to define as it must be to accomplish.

This type of literature, by these and lesser known authors, was widely published and read at the time young Sam Clemens commenced going to Sunday school. John Clemens, the author's father, is reported by Twain's biographer to have subscribed to *Peter Parley's Magazine* for the educational use of his children (more for moral than religious reasons), and thus there was ample opportunity for the author to have become familiar with these writings at an early age. Perhaps they were the first, among other things, to stir his moral concerns.

Speaking of this type of literature in his essay "On the Structure of *Tom Sawyer*," Walter Blair wrote in *Modern Philology* in August 1933, "Even when he skipped the sermons, the reader of a typical story had been able to get the point by noticing that the author's denouement observed the strictest poetic justice," so obvious was the intended purpose for the producing of such writings. The plots of most of these stories could have only appealed to those desiring their moral philosophies and religious beliefs confirmed by reading them.

A reaction was inevitable. According to Blair, "Beginning with the [eighteen] forties comic writers had sporadically beguiled readers with amoral portraits of unregenerated boys." Johnson J. Hooper, who gained a reputation with many as an immoral author for his low-minded humor, portrayed a creation named "Captain Simon Suggs" as an unquestionable rogue in an 1845 publication. Joseph Glover Baldwin followed in 1853 by adding "Simon Suggs, Jr., Esquire" to the literature. Such unruly characters were regularly rewarded in their adventures, while following the antithesis of what model boy literature preached.

Another series, one readily classed as a direct attack upon the model boy literature, featured as a central character a youth named "Ike" in stories about his aunt, the *Life and Sayings of Mrs. Partington*, tales collected in 1854. These stories by Benjamin Penhallow Shillaber, founder of the *Carpet Bag*, which circulated widely throughout the nation, projected a relationship with resemblances to the later *Tom Sawyer*. According to Blair, Ike was portrayed as "perhaps the most notorious of these juvenile delinquents," having "told lies, scratched letters on a newly japaned tray, broken countless windows, stolen oranges and cakes and doughnuts, hanged a cat, and imitated the hero of *The Black Avenger of the Spanish Main*." While other predecessors, including such as the adolescent "Sut Lovingood," created by George Washington Harris, are reflected in some part by Tom Sawyer in less specific ways, Shillaber's Ike appears to have exerted a direct influence on Mark Twain as he constructed his novel, although Tom is a much more fully realized character revealing greater inner character than Ike reveals.

The writing of these and other humorous authors are reflected in many instances in the work produced by Twain. Even while he was still young Sam Clemens, he probably read as many of their stories as opportunities permitted, and possibly continued rereading his favorites for years. The connections with most of the others, however, seem vague when compared to the author's relationship to Shillaber's work. The evidence for the strong influence of Shillaber's stories is additionally reinforced by the fact that the first of Twain's writings to appear outside of Hannibal appeared in Shillaber's magazine, *The Carpet Bag*. The younger author had every opportunity to read the stories about Ike and his aunt, developing what seems to have been a special attachment for them according to an essay by H.W. Mott, Jr., "The Origin of Aunt Polly," found in *Publishers Weekly* of 1938. A point of this essay is that the portrait of Ike's harassed aunt, Ruth Partington, used as an illustration in the 1854 collection of stories, bears an unmistakable resemblance to a portrait of Tom Sawyer's Aunt Polly as she appears in the final illustration of the American first edition of *The Adventures of Tom Sawyer*. The resemblance of one to the other is so remarkable that the result could hardly have been accidental. How this came about has never been explained, but Twain's mother, in certain photographs, shows a close likeness to the portrayals of the women in these two illustrations. It suggests the possibilities of being a private joke that Twain arranged, conceiving it for the benefit of his mother, still alive when *Tom Sawyer* was published. Nor are there only the pictorial similarities to suggest a connection between these women in Twain's mind, but when writing about his mother in one instance the author assigned deeds to her that actually belong to the fictitious Ruth Partington. Again it is not known if this was done by accident or otherwise. Thus, more than just pure coincidence appears to link Tom's Aunt Polly to Jane Clemens, she to Ruth Partington, aunt of young Ike who bears a resemblance to Tom Sawyer, who in turn resembles young Clemens.

Drawing what he found useful from the many humorous authors and their stories which he must have read, Twain's unique interpretations of similar materials are clearly never copies, even when the source seems obvious. Whatever he used always was thoroughly integrated, blended, and then filtered through his own extensive background before it reappeared in his unique style of wit and burlesque.

All this is surely a part of the evolution of his bad child theme, as opposed to the good child cliché, as it developed into a part of *Tom Sawyer*. Twain wrote several items using this theme during his first years as a professional writer. Those which demonstrate his reactions to the model child literature, all highly individualistic performances, are "Advice to Little Girls" (1865), "The Story of a Bad Little Boy" (1865), and "The Story of the Good Little Boy" (1870). Each of these uses patterns typical of the literature but done in opposition to the model boy theme; each features a burlesque approach, the approach favored in so many of his early sketches, weighted with clear-cut exaggerations. None brought any great increase of attention to their author, but the latter two were thought of highly enough by their author for them to be collected in his *Sketches, New and Old* (1875) and the first two point out clearly that Twain entertained thoughts of countering the model child image long before his attention was brought to it again in December of 1869 by reading Thomas Bailey Aldrich's *The Story of a Bad Boy*.

While the subject matter had a strong appeal for him, Twain could not endure Aldrich's prose style, telling his soon-to-be wife in a letter, "...for the life of me I could not admire the volume much." It may have been only a few months later that he tried unsuccessfully to write his own version of the material, using items from his own past, treating them in the first person as Aldrich had done, but leaning heavily on the burlesque style, when he sketched out his "Boy's Manuscript." While it seems that Twain was offended by the sentimentalisms he found in Aldrich's prose, he admired Aldrich's wit, and recognized the importance of Aldrich to the Eastern society. Twain's first meeting with him was in November 1871, though they had corresponded some months previous to that, and while Twain acceded to Aldrich's position in that society, he would always bear a hostility toward the man. At the time the Thomas Bailey Aldrich Memorial Museum was dedicated in 1908, Twain dictated into his autobiography this opinion of Aldrich: "his prose was diffuse, self-conscious, and barren of style."

However, in spite of the objections that Twain reserved for the writing style of Aldrich, *The Story of a Bad Boy* must have had a strong part in helping to stir up strong recollections of his own youth, and was a part of the reason he finally tried his own hand at writing about it. As is the case with *Tom Sawyer*, there is much evidence that Aldrich got a substantial part of his *The Story of a Bad Boy* material from his own boyhood, even going so far as to name his chief character and narrator "Tom Bailey." Aldrich wrote in the opening chapter, "I call my story the story of a bad boy, partly to distinguish myself from those faultless young gentlemen who generally figure in narratives of this kind, and partly because I was *not* a cherub." True to this word, Aldrich's boy was very different from the model boy touted by the moralists striving to mold characters by a distortion of reality. The antics assigned to Tom Bailey are distinctly not those of a model boy.

Clearly, the low-key humor and the lack of the double-barreled approach of burlesque style in the writing caused Twain to be as critical of the book as he was of its author. There exists, however, a close relationship between *The Story of a Bad Boy* and parts of *Tom Sawyer*. Because of a number of striking resemblances between these two books in certain parts, the suggestion might be entertained that one of the origins of *Tom Sawyer* was a desire on the part of Twain to apply the burlesque treatment to similar material. This may well have been an effective motive in the writing of the early sketches that were blended into the first chapters of the novel. While these resemblances are obvious in certain instances in the first part of the book, they are only faint echoes in the later parts. Thus, while Aldrich's novel had an immediate effect on some of the material that went into *Tom Sawyer*, as Twain got deeper into his own more complex treatment of the subject, adding other themes and layers to the composition, the effect gave way to more distinctive concerns.

*The Story of a Bad Boy* was published at essentially the same time as Twain's *Innocents Abroad*, with Aldrich's book receiving much more limited attention on the whole nationally — although among that society to which Twain aspired, the two volumes were received almost equally. The success won by Aldrich was not ignored by Twain and could well have encouraged in him, if not formed, thoughts about using fiction to create an acceptable past in a similar fashion, having noted that it could overcome many of the restrictions placed on such material used as straight autobiography. Twain also realized that much of his own success came upon the publication of *Innocents Abroad*, a work itself largely blending autobiography with fiction and humor. Twain sensed that if he should resort to a revised presentation of boyhood experiences, properly dressed in humor, they would succeed like Aldrich's.

Thus, continuing to toy with certain ideas he had already experimented with earlier, being newly motivated to establish an acceptable past for himself, and urged by a slight degree of envy for the success that Aldrich had found with the bad boy theme, Twain was drawn into the process that would gradually lead to the writing of Tom Sawyer's exploits. At the start, when Twain wrote the "Boy's Manuscript," all of the various forces he required were still largely unfocused. During the time when he put that sketch aside and applied himself to work on *Roughing It* a metamorphosis took place. It was to take some time, but the process was to continue, slowly absorbing his early attention to varieties of popular humor, taking in certain of the elements of Cervantes' humor and theme, blending these with Dickens, mixing it all with the anti–model-boy theme and Aldrich's successful use of it. By the time he had finished his work on *Roughing It* and found that it was necessary to move back another step in time, he turned his attention to his Hannibal days. Aware that the material needed stronger plotting, he put the most valuable part, the personal material for growing up in Hannibal, aside and channeled the remaining resources into the beginning of *The Gilded Age*. Even when he went back to the Hannibal material and wrote the chapters that would make up *The Adventures of Tom Sawyer*, he halted because of a feeling he was not realizing his original intentions.

# 10. Return to Hannibal

Commenting on his boyhood home, during one of his rare and brief returns to Hannibal, Missouri, Mark Twain in 1902 reportedly said of his Hill Street house (now preserved as a shrine): "Seems to have grown smaller. A boy's home, you know, is such a mighty big place to him! If I were to come back here in ten years from now, I suppose it wouldn't look any bigger than a bird cage."

The house in which Tom Sawyer lives with his Aunt Polly, cousin Mary, and half-brother Sid in *The Adventures of Tom Sawyer* is furnished only a vague description to fill the simple needs of the story, but it apparently was the Hill Street house in Hannibal which Mark Twain had in mind as he wrote his novel. The author placed it in "St. Petersburg, Missouri." The geography of St. Petersburg is approximately the equal of Hannibal's. Hannibal, like its fictional counterpart, sits on the bank of the Mississippi River across from the Illinois shore. Glasscock's Island located nearby across the river reminds viewers of "Jackson's Island" where Tom and his friends visit on their adventures aboard the borrowed raft. Almost immediately to the north of the small house in which Sam Clemens lived in Hannibal is a steep hill called Holliday's Hill, much of it wooded and with many acres of wooded lands nearby, an exacting model for Tom's "Cardiff Hill" and the woods to which Tom retreated, playing out his Robin Hood fantasies. To the south of Hannibal across Bear Creek, in what was once the favorite picnic ground for the people of early Hannibal, there is a cave that presently is designated the Mark Twain Cave. This cave, which has had several names through the years, was commonly called "McDowell's Cave" during Clemens' teenage years, after its then owner, the strange Doctor McDowell. In the novel Tom and Becky, on a picnic outing, are lost in its counterpart, termed "McDougal's Cave."

Concentrating on these particular features, Hannibal, disguised by the author but identifiable, is seen as the model for Tom Sawyer's town. As young Sam Clemens, Mark Twain spent approximately 13 years in Hannibal, from 1839 through 1853, from the age of four until he was 17. The Clemens family resided in several different locations in the town during that time, spending most of the period following 1844 in the Hill Street house. They left if briefly in 1846, only to return a few months later in 1847, after the death of John Clemens, the author's father. Those in the household at that time with young Sam were his mother, Jane Clemens; his older sister, Pamela; and his younger brother, Henry. These are the equivalents of Tom, Aunt Polly, cousin Mary, and half-brother Sid. Except for those days he boarded elsewhere as an apprentice to a local printer, Twain spent the remaining days of his Hannibal

period there. Located immediately across Hill Street from it was a house
where young Annie Laurie Hawkins lived during those same years.
Laura Hawkins, the most remembered of girl friends young Twain had
in Hannibal, served as the model for Becky Thatcher, as confirmed by
the author himself.

Although the Hill Street house seemed so much smaller to the aged
author, it was the recollected town that seemed to shrink to a greater extent as the author, in his later thirties, wrote his novel. In Twain's youth
Hannibal was not nearly so small as St. Petersburg is made to appear.
Even when the Clemens family moved there in 1839 Hannibal already
had a reported population of 1,034; while some ten years earlier a mere
30 inhabitants had settled there. Although it would not continue to grow
as rapidly during the years of Mark Twain's boyhood, it had more than
doubled in size by 1850 when nearly 2,500 individuals made up the
population. These figures indicate that Hannibal was not the quiet,
small, idealized hamlet that is suggested for Tom Sawyer's village by the
author. The creative requirements of the story dictated the elimination
of many elements, stripping from it all unnecessary details. There was
much more activity and area to Twain's boyhood town than we are
permitted to glimpse in its recreation as St. Petersburg.

According to the account of Svend Petersen, in his article "Splendid
Days and Fearsome Nights," Twain used the summer of 1844, which is
the year the Clemens family first entered the newly built structure on
Hill Street, as the period of his novel. Although the time scheme of the
novel is limited by a one-summer boundary, the actual events that
suggested many of Tom's experiences in the novel occurred in various
years. During many of those immortal summers when Twain was living
his Tom Sawyer years as young Sam Clemens, Hannibal was the scene of
visible industry that is barely suggested for St. Petersburg. A list of
businesses established by 1847 is broad. Not only were there several
slaughterhouses and pork processing firms, but also tobacco warehouses,
a tannery and a distillery. Other businesses operating included cooper
shops, dry goods stores, commission houses, hardware stores, druggists,
grocers, tinners, tailor shops, taverns, booksellers, one sculptor and
other various odd commercial ventures. Also there were lawyers, doctors, ministers, and school teachers — these made notable by the novel
whereas the industrial and retail activity was only briefly hinted at. Both
time and town were compressed in designing the literary model.

In spite of its economic importance, readers of *Tom Sawyer* are
only minimally reminded that the steamboat was flourishing, vessels of
this type stopping at Hannibal on the average of three times a day, with
a steady stream of passengers disembarking, persons traveling from and
to all points. The steamboat trade brought most of Hannibal's business
activity at that time, handling among numerous varieties of commodities an estimated million and a quarter dollars worth of wheat,
hemp, and tobacco. Countless wagons daily came in on the roads
leading into Hannibal and then aboard a small ferry, of which we are
reminded in *Tom Sawyer*, sailing a regular course across the river to and

from Illinois. Regular visits to Hannibal brought scores of lecturers, entertainers of every sort, showboats and circuses during the summer months, and a steady stream of visitors that included a fair share of charlatans of every degree. Such a town would have experienced only a few tranquil hours on only a few unusual days.

For its age and location, there was a noteworthy amount of culture in Hannibal, although that of St. Petersburg is held almost to a Fourth of July celebration with a speech by a Missouri senator of note, and the graduation exercises at the school. Beyond a slight reference to a circus, entertainment in Tom Sawyer's town appears nearly absent except for the occasional funeral, or a picnic attended mostly by children. Twain, familiar with the constant legal hearings that Hannibal witnessed almost daily, since his father was involved in many as a Justice of the Peace, presents the novel's only trial as an uncommon event, though undoubtedly as dramatic as any the real village might have recalled.

Tom gives hints of being "bookish" in a limited fashion, but there is little reference in the novel to easy access to a source for books, no hint given of the enlightened Hannibal Library with its selective collection of over 400 volumes, organized and operated by culturally-minded citizens that included John Clemens, but it is doubtful that children had access to its shelves except through the aid of a parent. The odds favor that in any town the size of early Hannibal there could be found a substantial percentage of persons whose lives were enriched and progressive through an access to culture in many of its forms; but Tom Sawyer's hamlet compares favorably only to the more remote of frontier hamlets. It is understandable that most of the cultural events and opportunities would have remained inaccessible and meaningless to a child of Tom's suspected age and this permits the author of *Tom Sawyer* to report only the futile, unsophisticated side of the village, however much it is a distortion of the truer picture. Hannibal was, in innumerable ways, very superior to its fictional counterpart.

There were no fewer than two newspapers operating in Hannibal during most of those years of Twain's boyhood, and many others that arrived through mail subscriptions. Twain himself, during the last years of his life in Hannibal, was closely associated with the labors of producing newspapers in Hannibal. He began this phase as an apprentice with Joseph Ament's *Missouri Courier* at around 14, perhaps after delivering papers for some months. Following that apprenticeship, he joined his brother Orion in the publishing of the *Western Union*, a paper Orion had founded in September of 1850, and which later absorbed the Hannibal *Journal*. Many of his hours were first given to the dirty work of a "printer's devil," while he grew skilled at setting type and occasionally found time to invent news items. Yet, there is only a very brief notation alloted to the newspaper industry as a part of Tom's hometown.

St. Petersburg was, out of necessity, actually modeled after the real Hannibal only in a limited, literary sense. While the days of the events depicted in the novel can be counted as one summer, an extended summer during which the hero unaccountably seems to age several years, the author used no more of the real town to create the imagined one than that which might be captured on a dozen snapshots taken over a few days.

Hannibal actually was not the only model used for the creating of St. Petersburg. It is necessary to search beyond Hannibal to account for the abundance of rural scenes in *Tom Sawyer*. What seems to be a more likely source for that sort of simple atmosphere is the smaller, somewhat quiet village of Mark Twain's birth, Florida, Missouri, a stunted community located a short trip from Hannibal even in slower times. Florida was the raw, primitive frontier town to which John Clemens moved his young family from Tennessee. In Tennessee his cultured manner and his visionary mind had not matched the promises of his labor. Preceding John Clemens, his four children and his wife to the sparse settlement were his wife's father, sister, and brother-in-law, with their family. Florida in 1835 was a fledgling community, situated near the Salt River, consisting of about thirty homes scattered along two main dirt roads that crisscrossed in the center. The surrounding population supported only a few stores and mills. Approaching it, and for his first few years there, the fresh town furnished John Clemens new promises, but it was never to grow much beyond the size he first discovered it.

The brother-in-law, John Quarles, a roughened, robust, jolly, hard-working farmer saw a more realistic vision in the prospects for the area than had the more opportunistic, genial, less hardy, cultured new arrival, John Clemens. Clemens' original hopes, which he actively pursued for a time, that the small village could be turned into a center of commerce, had little chance to be realized from the day of his arrival. Immediately, but vainly, he entered into the business of trading general commodities, involved himself in local politics, dabbled in legal services, and was a leader of a plan to create a navigable stream out of the tiny Salt River. For John Clemens, his venture in Florida ended as another disheartening experience.

Thus, Florida, Missouri, became the birthplace of Samuel Langhorne Clemens, destined to become "Mark Twain" as an author. He was born there on November 30, 1835, about six months after his family arrived. He was a premature baby, conceived on the journey to Missouri, and able to survive the nearly hopeless conditions of his birth with uncommon luck and the tender loving care of the womenfolk of Florida. A scrawny, puny baby, he was called "Little Sam" by virtue of his frail physique. Somehow, he managed to overcome the disadvantages of his beginnings and had become an active, adventurous boy by the age of four when his father could no longer view a future for Florida and decided to move the family to the more promising river town, Hannibal.

Twain's father, by then known as "Judge Clemens" because he reportedly held such a position in Monroe County, Missouri, did not prosper any more successfully in Hannibal than he had in the smaller community. Mark Twain's "Uncle John" and "Aunt Patsy," however, remained in Florida for the remaining years of their lives, operating a successful and moderately prosperous farm, the uncle having been no less ambitious, but more worldly. It was to this farm that Sam Clemens regularly returned for most of the eight summers that followed his move to Hannibal, or until he was 12. It was the atmosphere surrounding these long summer visits, staying with the Quarles family on the farm outside of Florida, that Twain remembered often with nostalgia as he sat in his specially built study at Quarry Farm, near Elmira in New York, many summers later writing much of the manuscript of *Tom Sawyer*.

Readers of *The Adventures of Tom Sawyer* readily note from time to time the vivid hints of the extensively more rural community in many of the novel's descriptive passages: a result of those summer days. In parts of Twain's *Autobiography* memories of these return visits to Monroe County provides some of the author's most colorful writing. From the blacks there, who supplied much of the farm's labor, held yet as slaves in that period, he learned in detail of a wide range of superstitions (that are recalled in several writings, including *Tom Sawyer*) as these laborers gathered in the evenings to entertain themselves and the children around the farm. Twain later would often vividly recall the quiet countryside, the hush of the summer days when he sometimes attended the primitive school in Florida, or the tiny, rural church on Sundays. The impressions that these activities left with him were no less than the memory of the good food he ate and the robust nature of the Quarles family where he had witnessed much joy. His summer adventures at the Quarles farm, during a large portion of his Tom Sawyer years, were accompanied with hours of play with his cousins and renewed visits to nearby neighbors, many of whom had known him from the day of his birth. In all, he probably spent close to a third of the days of his boyhood in the vicinity of the town of his birth, these being especially the days of his summers, and these were the days he remembered best and recalled with the greatest respect.

Hannibal's geography may allow it preeminence as a model for the location of Tom Sawyer's activities, but the atmosphere of Tom's St. Petersburg is more a result of the rural Florida background. The fact that all the basic characters in the story originated mainly from models the author recalled from his Hannibal days, along with the geographical similarities of Hannibal, have served to obscure the important influence of the village of Florida.

Many people who had lived in Hannibal at the time of Twain's boyhood, from time to time attempted to establish personal claims for being a model of one or another of the characters in the novel, after the author had gained recognition and his *Tom Sawyer* novel had begun to win international fame. Twain's own recollections, and the research of others, reveals some of the names of individuals who were related in various ways to the Hannibal experiences of the author, but those who can be accurately designated as models for any character found in the novel are few compared to the available candidates. The lapse of time between his childhood and the period of the writing of the manuscript, plus the artistic license and the creative desire of the author, resulted in a blending and disguising that limited and confused the bits of material and models used for those sharing some contributions to the book. There is the possibility that persons who lived around Florida also served as models for characters in the novel, but the record holds little about them and consequentially little has been said.

Turning to speculation for a reason for the name given Tom's town, it is conceivable that the name symbolizes the idealized conditions and reflects the mysterious presence that hangs over the inhabitants, especially the more youthful members during selective summer hours — thus having a name suggestive of a heavenly city, not an earthly one.

But, while idealizing in one direction, Mark Twain is continually satirical and poking fun in another. The heavenly city is disturbed at intervals by the reality that surrounds those events which touch Tom's adventures. At certain moments when the town's tranquility is disturbed it becomes a darkened pit. The author, it appears, never offered a reason for his choice of the name (which he spelled variously in his original manuscript by sometimes adding an "h" at the end). However, the selection was a fortunate selection considering its powerful symbolic connotations. It may suggest, among other possibilities, a comparison of Tom's hamlet with the more widely known St. Petersburg, the once glittering capital of enigmatic Russia and the seat of czardom. Considering the many serious and moralistic threads woven into the background of the author's humor, such a reason for the choice might well apply. For whatever may be drawn from it, following only one day the publication of the article that suggested the cave local to Mark Twain, the same St. Louis newspaper carried an article, on page 2 of the April 8, 1874 issue, headlined: ST. PETERSBURG (RUSSIA). It was a travel letter written for the paper by Minister Marshall Jewell. If there is a good possibility that Twain subscribed to the *Democrat* and had seen the first article, could not the next day's headline have also influenced his novel? Whatever the reason for naming Tom's town "St. Petersburg," the name is an effective choice, allowing a satirical view, one both humorous and serious in terms of comparison.

While Twain suggested that to the man returning again to the house of his childhood, it seems so much smaller than it had to the boy, he may have hoped to suggest that a man can never really return to his boyhood town, not even in fiction. This may be the basis of why all his visits, whenever he made one of his rare return trips to Hannibal, were always brief. The illustrations had disappeared. The town he had thought he had viewed as a boy, much larger in so many ways than its literary counterpart, was never more than a boy's restricted vision.

# 11. "Drawn from Life"

Many look upon *Tom Sawyer* as an autobiographical novel. Whether this is true is an important question. Mark Twain has established a reputation, resulting largely from his style, that places him among the earlier "realist" authors of American literature. Certainly, in this book, Twain is a realist in the generally understood literary sense of the word and his novel is weighted with autobiographical material.

The book offers many hints that not only was Twain writing about a real boy, but that the character of "Tom Sawyer" was largely based upon himself. This is so even though in the "Preface" the author attempts to discourage the idea, declaring that among "the adventures recorded" which "really occurred," only "one or two" were his own. While admitting the "real" basis for the book, Twain's attempt to disguise his hero as a composite character is a flimsy diversion. His claim appears invalid for several reasons. One is that many more than "one or two" events of the novel fit biographical information about the author. Another is that Tom Sawyer, for all the fiction surrounding him, stays convincingly real.

There are a number of boys in literature that readers, caught up by the words on the pages of a book, honestly can relate to. Some have related this way to Tom Bailey in Aldrich's *The Story of a Bad Boy* — although, if Twain can be believed, Aldrich's presentation did not arouse him. One who did react positively to Aldrich's Tom Bailey, and again to Twain's Tom Sawyer, was William Dean Howells. Howells wrote, "In a word he [Tom] is a boy." Millions of readers have had similar feelings concerning Tom Sawyer. Only a few readers might feel he is not realistically drawn.

Tom Sawyer is undoubtedly a dynamic literary character. His reputation derives from the fact that he is notable for lying, trading, playing hooky, frustrating his family and teachers, and frustrating the entire community by running off to "drown" and returning for his own "funeral." He is both a doer and a dreamer, his head filled with an array of romantic adventurous tales and unpredictable schemes. Yet, his family loves him and his friends are continually loyal — as are most readers. Tom wins admirers because he dramatically falls in love, then proves himself through an impressive act of heroism.

A practical reason for a strong interest in the character of Tom Sawyer is that he was modeled upon his creator as a boy, a fact that does not necessarily mean his adventures are autobiographical. There is a great amount of fiction allotted the character, although Twain saw Tom Sawyer as himself, young Sam Clemens. All authors, to greater or lesser degrees, draw from their own experience some of the factors applied to

the characters they create. This is especially true for their chief characters. While some strive carefully to separate themselves as greatly as
possible, others (such as Thomas Wolfe, for one) make only the most
feeble efforts to disguise the origin of their heroes. We know that Twain
deliberately drew upon material from his own boyhood to create his
hero, because as the character was originally conceived, the author had
a strictly personal reason among his several reasons, the creation of an
acceptable past for himself in his new social surroundings. This factor,
important at the start, became less important as time went on. As he felt
it less important, it allowed him to turn more to true fiction, as he did in
the last half of his story.

In the novel, Twain finally chose to give the reader almost nothing
regarding Tom's history before or after the events of the book. Yet,
because of the writer's genius, Tom is readily accepted by most as a
complete and "real" character. Tradition alone has furnished him with a
tattered straw hat (that of the novel being a "speckled straw hat" reserved for Sundays), along with his checkered shirt, suspenders and
ragged overalls that reach just below his knees. Most of what we are told
about Tom's clothing is gathered through brief hints, often given as contrasts. Likewise, he is never described physically as being fat or thin, or
short or tall, although tradition again has supplied generous freckles;
carrot-colored, curly hair; small, intensive eyes and a lithe body. Each
of the many illustrators of various editions of *Tom Sawyer* have added
their own variations, each creating their own idealized version of the
young hero.

While the words describing him physically are rare, the reader sees
him by means of the things he does, running, climbing fences, descending from a second floor bedroom, enduring harsh punishment, rafting,
swimming, and crawling courageously to freedom from the tomb-like
cave. In spite of the dearth of description we are given about Tom
Sawyer, the reader sees him exactly as the author wanted him to be
seen — poor in worldly possessions, but a free spirit, a normal boy rich
with imagination.

While we are given Twain's statement at the front of the book as a
"Preface," it is more as an *afterthought* since it was written long after he
began the book and more likely near the time he had finally considered it
finished. After nearly five years of wrestling with his identity problem,
Mark Twain had by then reached a point where its importance had
diminished; thus he chose to modestly disclaim his relationship to Tom:

> Most of the adventures recorded in this book really occurred; one
> or two were experiences of my own, the rest those of boys who were
> schoolmates of mine. Huck Finn is drawn from life; Tom Sawyer
> also, but not from an individual — he is a combination of the char-
> acteristics of three boys whom I knew, and therefore belongs to the
> composite order of architecture.

His focus on Huckleberry Finn's origins while blurring Tom's suggests a clever trick, a keen psychological insight, since there is a tendency to believe more strongly what is skillfully denied. While this preface pleads validity, it is nevertheless a mixture of truth, declared and camouflaged, the various parts needing to be weighed.

The opening declaration of the Preface, "Most of the adventures recorded in this book really occurred," is inaccurate. At least 50 percent, if not more, of the adventures of Tom are pure invention. Surrounded by imaginary events and distorted through the many necessary acts of creativity, those few adventures that *really* occurred are sufficiently historical that they refute the author's "one or two were experiences of mine." They range well above the admitted number. These then indicate that Tom Sawyer is basically, though not totally, young Sam Clemens. The adventures that are most definitely based on real events are dominant in parts of the book's opening chapters, while the remaining adventures are almost totally fictional, dominating the last half of the novel. Only the most remote connections exist between these fictional adventures and Twain's boyhood experiences. They come, however, only after Twain had established by the use of personal material that he was writing about himself when he invented Tom. It was a clever feint to claim that "the rest" of the adventures were "those of boys who were schoolmates of mine."

Whatever Mark Twain's schoolmates did contribute to the book appear to be generalities. Twain's language is misleading when he follows the statement — one with a large degree of truth — "Huck Finn is drawn from life," with a statement that is only partially accurate, "Tom Sawyer also, but not from an individual...." The claim that Tom "is a combination of the characteristics of three boys I knew, and therefore belongs to the composite order of architecture" is a distortion whose only reason had to be an attempt at disguise. By the time he realized that the novel was to be published, he had reconsidered his original intentions. Of course it is inevitable that some of the boys Sam Clemens had sometimes closely associated with as he grew up may have influenced certain of the invented characteristics of Tom Sawyer. Most details, however, were borrowed generously from his own image.

Numerous newspaper items, interviews, articles in magazines and journals, and parts of various books add to the extensive list of names of individuals whose lives touched the events of Twain's youth in Hannibal. There are no fewer than 30 boys, and half as many girls, all having played various roles on different occasions according to their accounts, or the accounts of others. While this seems to complicate the process of elimination, of all individuals named only a few can accurately be classed as potential models for any of the chief characters in the book. None of the various listings of names, including those by Twain, are completely reliable — though certain individuals have been named frequently.

First in any list, Will Bowen, Mark Twain's "First, & Oldest & Dearest Friend," certainly shared with the author many of the original events that form the basis for Tom Sawyer's adventures after discounting the embellishments of fiction. The letter the author sent Bowen in 1870 is the strongest evidence of this, and it is supported by other statements and facts. The bond between the two remained intact with few lapses until Bowen's death. Bowen is second only to the author as a possible model for any of the characteristics or adventures assigned to the fictional hero. Evidence indicates he probably spent many hours with young Sam Clemens, hours shared at times with Will's brothers, Sam and Bart. Their comaraderie had a strong place in Twain's recollections of growing up in Hannibal.

Also prominent as a companion to Sam Clemens and most frequently named as the model for "Joe Harper" was John Briggs. John Garth, another long standing member of the "gang," could lay a claim to having been the third member of the triumvirate cited as the model for Tom Sawyer. Beyond these few — boys who played any occasional part in the Hannibal experiences, according to Twain's autobiographical writings and other records — chances are slender that any could establish a strong claim as a model for any characteristics associated with the novel's hero. Some among these others, however, were used as models in differing degrees for lesser and indistinct characters that fill out the background of the novel.

One other boy, and eventually the most important of Twain's childhood companions in a literary sense, was Tom Blankenship. He existed on the fringes of the gang, joining them often in those activities connected with the nearby river, hunting, fishing, swimming, boating, and exploring. Unlike the others, Tom Blankenship never attended school or went to church. He came from a family not only more poverty stricken than Twain's own, but lacking in all of the genteel qualities of the Clemenses. The reputation of the Blankenship family was of such poor quality that parents commonly forbid their children to associate with any of its members. Yet, many did, including young Twain, and to Tom Blankenship alone he gave the honor of being the key model for Huckleberry Finn. In dress and habits this youngster was a close duplicate of Tom Sawyer's closest companion. Tom Blankenship, like Huck Finn, smoked; his father was recognized as a drunkard; and his speech undoubtedly was a rough usage of fresh Missouri dialect. Unlike Huck Finn, however, he had a number of brothers and sisters. They all resided in a large, ramshackle house near to the rear of the Clemenses' Hill Street house. Other than Tom, only the older brother, Benson, serving as a model for some of the characteristics of "Muff Potter," is ever cited as having influenced the author.

Although young Tom Blankenship served as the original model, in actuality Huckleberry Finn is a composite character when all details are recognized. The last name was adopted by the author from another of the town's recognized drunkards, Jim Finn. The first name, or nickname probably, so fittingly selected for this character, has an elusive origin. While huckleberries flourish in the wilds of most eastern states, they are not claimed to be native to Missouri. It is obvious that many of the original settlers of that state came from places where they did abound and their reputation likely traveled with these individuals, but Twain's only use of the name occurred after the author had grown familiar with the aspects of the eastern states' culture where huckleberries are widely popular. If it had been applied to any individual even as a nickname, such an event does not appear in the records. The suitability of the name for the character, is one of Twain's most visible exhibits of literary genius.

Huck is next to Tom in importance to *The Adventures of Tom Sawyer*. He became even more important for his creator as the chief character of the author's more highly rated novel, *The Adventures of Huckleberry Finn*. Once this character is broadened, as in the second book, the true composite nature of his origin becomes clear. A number of critics have observed the alter ego factor involved in Huck's origin. While Tom Sawyer represents the cultured, romantic, restrained side of Mark Twain, a side yearning to break free, Huck Finn symbolizes his opposite qualities as a rebel, wanderer, and realist. Frank Baldanze, in *Mark Twain: An Introduction*, described it this way: "In contrast between the bragging, bullying, romantically ingenious and inventive Tom and the uncombed, unshod unregenerate child of the woods and the docks as represented by Huck, we have a dichotomy that must represent two very profound aspects of Clemens' own nature."

While Twain drew upon certain of his childhood companions for bits of the original characteristics of Tom Sawyer and Huckleberry Finn, he found their more distinguishing characteristics within his own life and mind. Twain is the prime model. Although in the process of creating his fiction the lines have been blurred, we see aspects of Twain that are only minutely treated in the books of autobiography and biography. This makes the details doubly important and helps to account for the aura of sharp reality about them. Somehow, in his erratic method of creating fiction, Twain was able to distill the qualities vital to the proper formation and description of these two contrasting types, and important to an understanding of his own genius.

The other characters of the *Tom Sawyer* novel are more frequently found forming caricatures of the individuals who served as their models. Henry Clemens, the author's younger brother, served as the model for "Sid," Tom's half brother. Twain removed any doubt there may have been about this in his *Autobiography*. He said of Henry Clemens, "He is Sid in Tom Sawyer." This and other items tie young Sam Clemens and his brother to several occurrences recollected from life that appear as parts of the novel. The incident of Sid calling the aunt's attention to the color of the thread Tom used to resew his collar together duplicates one which trapped young Sam Clemens because of Henry's sharpness and integrity. The material regarding the stolen sugar and the broken bowl was another designed from a similar one in which the brothers had actually been involved. The fights between Sid and Tom repeat actual spats that arose between the dissimilar brothers. Twain, knowing he had caricatured Henry, concluded his autobiographical statement, conscientiously explaining "But Sid was not Henry. Henry was a very much finer and better boy than ever Sid was." Perhaps this partly explains why the author designated Sid only as Tom's half brother.

Twain's sister, Pamela, a full eight years older than the author, was always somewhat more serious minded, as their father had been. Like Tom's cousin "Mary," Pamela spent short periods traveling away from the family's home in order to earn money giving music lessons, and whenever present with the family she would take over the duties of aiding her reluctant brother with his preparations for the Sunday school. It was this relationship that the author recalled and depicted as the close relationship of Tom to Mary. Such use of actual incidents, often built on limited recollections, eliminated more material than they used.

Such a process of elimination is true also of the use made of Twain's father and mother in designing those characters suggested by them in the novel. In a sense, Twain denied the existence of his father, making his hero an orphan, then substituting a satirically conceived caricatured father — at a distance — in the figure of "Judge Thatcher," a character whose residence Twain was often uncertain of in different parts of the novel. Initially, he is described as an important person from a *distant* place, "twelve miles," where the court house has a "tin roof." John Clemens was an aloof man, vainly concerned with his personal dreams of elusive success, primarily interested in gaining recognition for himself as being a step above his fellow common men, proud of his ability to handle legal matters with an air of dispatch, a gentleman — but an apparent failure as a father. He exerted great efforts to fit himself into the part he believed destiny had reserved for him, always at the expense of his family. Judge Clemens' love of learning gave him certain advantages, but these did not suffice to overcome the boundless enthusiasm he had for shortcuts to financial and personal goals. In the book *Mark Twain at Work*, the critic Bernard DeVoto points out, "The Judge ends by swallowing Lawyer Thatcher..."; Twain unconsciously allowed the interpretation that he had drawn both characters from the same model.

Mark Twain's description of Judge Thatcher as a "middle-aged man ... a prodigious personage — no less than a county judge — altogether the most august creation these children ever looked upon — and they wondered what kind of material he was made of — and they half wanted to hear him roar, and were half afraid he might, too," provides an excellent caricature of his father. It is a deft recognition, accurate to a point, but severely limited — approaching his father timidly as he always did in the course of his infrequent writing about him. At this point in the novel, as if feeling traces of guilt for the act of caricature, Twain depicts Tom showing off in Sunday school, preparing for a moment of triumph before his peers, anticipating the illegal award of a Bible, and leading to an introduction to Judge Thatcher — only to embarrass himself at the final moment by incorrectly answering a simple question asked by the Judge.

Twain indicated more obvious respect for his mother, Jane Clemens, and thus his caricature of her as "Aunt Polly" is perhaps less severe than others, being on the whole an accurate description of his mother and her manners, though nevertheless poking fun as a caricature does through overemphasis. She was a stronger, more forceful, more earthy person than his father. A woman of high spirits and broad compassion, she maintained her marital duties with dignity, bearing silently the failures of her husband, never openly reflecting the restrictions it placed upon her life. Even during the difficult years before his father died, it was his mother who preserved the family. She provided the religious training, administered the daily authority that governed all the practical matters of raising children, the feeding, the clothing, and the nursing. After the death of her husband, Jane Clemens quietly accepted the full responsibilities of her position and saved the family from total disaster. She played her role with cunning wisdom, balanced by love and discipline, and never totally relinquished the position of family head until her final years.

That her characteristics provided the materials Twain used in originating Aunt Polly in *Tom Sawyer* is plain to most observers. In his biography, Albert Bigelow Paine states it is an absolute fact, saying, "Jane Clemens was the original of Tom Sawyer's 'Aunt Polly,' and her portrait as presented in that book is considered perfect." Her creation as an aunt could have resulted from the fact that many of Twain's river companions, that he brought home during his days as a pilot, generally called his mother "Aunt Jane." Unlike his writing in the "Boy's Manuscript" where Billy Rogers has a mother, who also "worries" about him as Tom's aunt does, in writing *Tom Sawyer* the author seems to have stepped back to widen his canvas. Because Twain knew, only too well, that he had inherited and learned much of his ability to deal with humor through his mother, there is a great deal of love in the portrayal — although Aunt Polly is continually deceived and confounded by her errant nephew, much as was a part of the real life relationship of mother and son in his boyhood.

Still, there exists a possibility that to a slight degree Aunt Polly was a composite character and not wholly Mark Twain's outline of his mother. He was very close to his real aunt, Martha Ann Quarles (called "Aunt Patsy" by all), she being like a second mother to young Sam Clemens during the days spent at his Uncle John's farm. She and his mother were sisters and no doubt shared some qualities. Also, among those he would have visited in Florida, Missouri, was Polly Ann Buchanan, who claimed the honor of having put the first garment on him as a premature infant, possibly never tiring of reminding him and deserving of an honorary title as "Aunt Polly." These all must share with Twain's long time knowledge and appreciation of Benjamin P. Shillaber's fictional creation, "Mrs. Ruth Partington," who suffered the tricks of her nephew "Ike" much in the fashion of the later Tom Sawyer. His extended attention to this character deserves consideration in any determination of the origins of Aunt Polly — yet, all the others together, would add little to the characteristics of Aunt Polly that Jane Clemens had not already supplied.

Mark Twain's memory of growing up in Hannibal did not center entirely on his family life and his boyhood games and adventures. It included, somewhat more centrally than he was willing to verify, an early and long childhood romance with a neighbor girl living almost directly across Hill Street. Annie Laurie Hawkins was exclusively the model for Tom Sawyer's sweetheart, "Becky Thatcher." Almost all of the *Tom Sawyer* narrative which centers on what takes place between Tom and Becky has a basis in actual events that occurred between Sam Clemens and Laura Hawkins, with the chief exception being that they were never really lost in the local cave at any time. That event was almost totally invented. They had gone on picnics together at the same grounds where the cave's model was located; they at times attended school and church together; he had carried Laura's books; and the author, having among his characteristics many that Tom was granted, including a propensity to show-off, had often performed antics in the Tom Sawyer fashion to win Laura's attention.

Laura Hawkins had a singular place in Twain's childhood and thereafter for many years, longer perhaps than factual evidence makes apparent. Although there was no correspondence between them from the time he left Hannibal, to return only for brief, rare visits, until they corresponded again late in life, many years after the writing of *Tom Sawyer*, the author was never able to completely put his first romantic experiences out of his mind. He cherished the wealth of memories from his childhood days in Hannibal with exceptional pride, his memories of Laura a special treasure that he guarded with uncommon protection. Though nearly 18 years passed after leaving Hannibal, and he was a newly married man in his middle thirties when writing to Will Bowen in 1870, Twain gave special emphasis to his recollections by including at the end the stated fact that "Laura Hawkins was my sweetheart."

Laura appears in the "Boy's Manuscript" as Billy Roger's sweetheart Amy. Although the origins of a chief female character in the novel *The Gilded Age* that Twain wrote with Warner are of greater complexity, the author drawing upon recollections of another Laura who had captured his attention for a brief span during his pilot days on the river (perhaps as much for her name as for her young beauty), and a third Laura from San Francisco who had gained notoriety in the newspapers near the time of the writing of that novel (her name and deeds fitting the needs of the novel's plot), it was the original Laura that was in Twain's mind when the character was first conceived and the corresponding name, "Laura Hawkins," was applied. The final ending of Laura in *The Gilded Age* would indicate a somewhat confused and complex attitude toward the various Lauras serving as models. There is no "Laura" used in *Tom Sawyer*, but Tom does "jilt" an "Amy" as his former romantic interest when he is overcome with interest in Becky Thatcher. In creating Becky, Mark Twain may have caricatured some of his model's traits and dress, but he did not manage to overcome his deep and lingering devotion. Disguising but never obliterating the essential events, the author preserved that early romance in the fashion he wanted.

It also followed him more secretly to the end of his life, and even while he presented on one hand a Victorian image to the public as

Samuel Langhorne Clemens, he was simultaneously an ambiguous figure in his character as Twain, the shrewd author, youthfully in love with the ideal little neighbor girl, as Tom Sawyer had been portrayed — always aware of her true being, her secret thoughts and potentials as a woman. Laura Hawkins and her surrogate successors continued to maintain a place in his world during all of its successive stages. Laura Wright, the reportedly attractive teenage girl he fell in love with for a time during his piloting days on the Mississippi; Olivia Langdon at the time of their courtship when she was a frail, innocent girl just out of her teens; his close devotion to his own daughters through their childhood years; and his attentions in his final decade devoted to several young girls he termed "angel fish"; all these indicate the intensity at which his childhood affair continued to reappear in his adult life. When Twain finally saw Laura Hawkins again, and for the last time, in 1908 at his Stormfield home, some 55 years separated from their Hannibal childhood, she was (according to Paine) "Laura Frazer now, widowed and in her seventies, with a granddaughter already a young lady quite grown." Reality had demonstrated the taking of its toll, the vision had undergone several revisions, but it had never vanished. Becky was momentarily again with Tom.

In the search for the models of those characters of *Tom Sawyer* "drawn from life," it is worth recalling what Paine recorded in his *Mark Twain: A Biography* where the 71-year-old author is reported as having said, "Speaking of companions ... after fifty years ... of my playmates I recall John Briggs, John Garth, and Laura Hawkins — just those three; the rest I buried long ago, and memory cannot even find their graves." Whether that statement is more symbolic than honest needs to be considered. Memory plays tricks — it is sometimes based on fact, sometimes on fantasy. Yet such a memory could have a significance beyond its intent. While Twain claimed not to remember any longer the others who had touched his life in Hannibal and became models for characters in *Tom Sawyer*, investigations of his writings and other reliable sources reveal additional characters that can be matched to the names of several persons.

The widow of Captain Richard Holliday, who lived in Hannibal's equivalent of a mansion on Holliday's Hill, was appropriated as a model for the "Widow Douglas" of the novel. John Davies, a Hannibal bookseller, entered the novel as "Mr. Jones" or the "Welshman" by way of his relation to real events not dissimilar to those in which that character is involved. "Alfred Temple," the new boy Tom dislikes and licks, was modeled upon a Jim Reagan who arrived fresh from St. Louis and dressed much in the manner of the fictional counterpart. The "model boy" title belongs to "Willie Mufferson," a character modeled upon Theodore Dawson, son of Twain's last schoolmaster, the schoolmaster who became the model for "Dobbins," Tom's schoolmaster. The briefly seen young black boy, who appears at the opening of the "whitewashing" chapter, was based on a young slave Judge Clemens retained on a rental basis, recalled one place in other writings by Mark Twain as

"Sandy" and elsewhere as "Lewis." The "aged and needy postmaster, who had seen better days," briefly noted, found his origin in Hannibal's postmaster, Abner Nash. Becky's cousin "Jeff" takes his name from Laura Hawkins' brother Jeff, who died as a child. The originals of "Doc Robinson" and "Injun Joe," as well as the remaining characters in *Tom Sawyer*, appear to be drawn in part on actual models in young Sam Clemens' town, but identifying individuals for these remains difficult and clouded by rumor and unrealistic claims. Although Twain created much of the basic story out of events similar to those in his own childhood, and peopled it with characters that are unmistakably based on people he once knew — in the final creative act he selected only those characteristics that served the purpose of his art.

While *Tom Sawyer* cannot lay an unreserved claim to the term "autobiographical fiction," readers usually relate to Tom as they might relate to any *real* boy. This happens although Tom Sawyer is an enigma, undermining our understanding even as he fascinates us, giving us only the barest details upon which to launch our imagination, as he wins our sympathy and weaves himself into acceptance in our knowledge. Was it a mere stroke of luck for a novelist who employed a seemingly haphazard technique that produced this enigma — or, was it sheer genius won from hours of practice and protracted labor? How much of the work's success derives from the autobiographical strength of the contents of the opening chapters that were then reinforced by the more imagined and mature events of the climax?

The status of *The Adventures of Tom Sawyer* as a classic derives more perhaps from the creation of its chief hero as a real boy than from any other factor that can be isolated.

# Part III

*After Publication*

# 12. Editions of *Tom Sawyer*

Since *Tom Sawyer* was published, it has enjoyed a popularity comparable to few other books — a reputation earned against tremendous odds. Most books reach obscurity a relatively short time after they are published. Of those few that enjoy popularity, in nearly all cases it is short-lived. A handful of books receive a limited reception that continues among special classes. The few books which are published and then remain in print for several decades, read by individuals with a sincere interest in literature, form yet another level. Those rare items that remain in print and are continually read by millions of average readers for anything over a hundred years are indeed a singular group. Mark Twain's *Tom Sawyer* is in a high position even among these.

Since its first publication in 1876, *Tom Sawyer* has never been out of print, and has been reissued many times in a wide variety of editions by numerous publishers. The total number of these editions range into the hundreds, the number of copies printed and sold totaling into the millions. These include a variety of editions illustrated by a variety of artists depicting the characters in many different styles. It includes the many translations of the novel into foreign languages which have provided the book a universal recognition seldom matched. Despite those barriers imposed by differing languages and cultures, the book's chief characters have gained a wide literary reputation. Although the book's popularity advanced slowly at first, then at an increasing pace for a number of decades, that popularity has only recently leveled off, but still shows no sign of any decline in the immediate future. While a million new titles may be published by the beginning of the 21st century, *Tom Sawyer* should remain an item found on as many bookshelves as it is today, or perhaps even more. Literary critics may argue the classical status it deserves, but its extended popularity with readers from the time of its first edition is a matter of record that must be dealt with by all who judge it.

It may seem strange that the first publication of *Tom Sawyer* appeared some 4,400 miles from Hannibal, Missouri, or almost 3,400 miles from Hartford, Connecticut, but it is what the author wanted. Twain and his English agent, Moncure Conway, believed that to secure a copyright of any value in England, the novel had to be published there first. There were strong legal reasons for this action, and if the English edition could have been followed immediately by the American edition, matters would have worked out more rewarding for the author. Six months elapsed, however, between the two editions during which an unauthorized Canadian publisher chose to circumvent the English copyright law, issuing a "pirated" edition of the work with type set from the English printing. Thus thousands of readers in Canada and many in the United States were able to purchase and read *Tom Sawyer* before Mark Twain's principle publisher, the American Publishing Company, presented its first edition. The Canadian pirate publisher was enriched, but paid the book's author not one cent in royalties.

There is no protesting the fact that the authentic first edition of *The Adventures of Tom Sawyer* was that issued by Chatto and Windus in London on June 8, 1876. Chronologically deserving the title of "First Edition" in all respects, it is now generally known as the "English first edition." Frugal and totally undistinguished, it consisted of 341 numbered pages. It contained no illustrations, and was bound in red cloth-covered boards standing about 20 centimeters high. Evident in its make-up are certain signs of hasty production. It was issued as a general trade edition, competitively priced and thoroughly plain according to the standards of American subscription publications. The edition was most likely designed in this manner because it was intended to be an item for sale in the retail bookshops scattered throughout Great Britain where many titles vied for recognition among readers who had little to spend. The type from which it was printed was set using the copyist's copy of the manuscript that Conway had personally carried with him upon a return trip to England from America.

For this reason the text of the English edition inherited some variations from the text of the American edition, incorporated unwittingly because of a number of differences, most of a relatively minor nature, allowed to prevail in the two manuscripts through the carelessness of the author. There are some differences, however, mostly in the numbering of the chapters, in the English first edition which are the fault of the publisher, being among those signs indicating the hasty preparations. In the English first edition there are two chapters numbered "x," while none is numbered "xi." Then there are two chapters numbered "xii," the second of which should have been "xiii." The chapter which should have borne "xiv," was numbered "xiii," with the true xv designated as "xiv," and xvi as "xv." What serves as Chapter "xvi" for the English edition actually derives from the final part of the American edition's Chapter xvi beginning "About midnight Joe awoke, and called the boys."

Chapter numbers agree for the next four chapters, but then a second in the English edition is numbered "xx" (this being "xxi" of the American), and the numbers of the remaining chapters are consequently numbered one lower than comparable chapters in the American edition. The result is that the final chapter in the English edition is numbered "xxxiv" but there are actually 36 chapters against the American edition's 35 (a result of the additional chapter minus two missing numbers, "xi" and "xxv"). Some of this mixup was a result of Twain's juggling of chapters and followed from his various numberings of them (e.g., among the most outstanding changes apparent is in numbering "Chapter 10," which he first made "9," then "9½," and finally "10," as he revised, changing also many manuscript page numbers and adding pages to the chapter).

The English publishers, however, must be faulted because they seem not to have made any effort to check and correct the obviously erroneous numbers, as set up by their printers, assigning them numbers in the proper order. The extra chapter in the English edition ("XVI") was probably a correct rendering of Twain's original wishes, the difference being an error made later on the part of True Williams. The illustrator of the American edition misread the original manuscript numbering, which he used when sketching his illustrations for the head of each chapter, these being drawings incorporating the chapter numbers. This mistake allowed two chapters to be run together, an error the author discovered while checking the final proof sheets, but considered not worth the trouble to correct (the only change then necessary being the Table of Contents providing that it had already been set up in type). Such things might be disturbing to anyone with a desire for exactitude, but they have no effect upon the story itself.

The English edition, first in terms of time, was followed closely by the pirate edition produced in Canada by Belford Brothers of Toronto. This printing of the novel appeared on or about July 29, 1876, being copied from the English edition which had arrived there and had gone on sale a week earlier. This happened while Twain was less than 250 miles away, spending his summer at Quarry Farm, just outside of Elmira, New York. Although he was aware of and concerned with the threat of his work being stolen by a pirate publisher, evidence indicates the first knowledge of this happening came to him only several months later.

Supposedly, the English edition was protected by the Imperial copyright law and the Canadian publishers were probably proceeding illegally, although they argued otherwise. Twain and his English agent, Conway, had trustingly expected that the English copyright would suffice, but the Candian publishers based their right to reprint the book upon the fact that the publishers had not copyrighted the work in Canada. According to correspondence from Twain to Conway dated December 9, 1876, the author had believed "all the necessary steps had been taken" by Chatto and Windus to copyright the work in Canada. Either the legalities meant nothing to the pirate publishers; or the copyright had been applied for, but delayed by bureaucratic procedures; or was applied for only after the problem arose—otherwise Chatto and Windus had misinformed the author. It is by no means a clear issue, but it would seem that the English publisher strongly relied on the Imperial copyright to hold in any British controlled area, at least until the formalities of a copyright could be completed. It appears that the only reasonable solution would have been for Chatto and Windus to have published an edition there under their imprint to insure an ironclad copyright in Canada. Such a method was not totally uncommon, nor had Belford Brothers always reprinted items coming out in England first without authorization from the original publishers, but in this case it was bypassed for reasons unstated.

Had he used the court in Canada and obtained an injunction again-the unauthorized publication of the novel, Twain very likely could have stopped further distribution of it but, by the time he was aware of what had occurred, thousands of copies had been printed and sold. The penalties for illegal publication were minor compared with the rewards. At the time of *Tom Sawyer*'s publication the laws remained unclear and many instances of piracy were taking place almost daily in both Canada and England, as well as in this country. Uncertain of the outcome of legal action, Twain realized there was not much to gain in pursuing the matter.

The earliest indication that Twain knew of the Canadian publication appears in a letter to Moncure Conway dated November 2, 1876. "Belford Bros., Canadian thieves are flooding America with a cheap pirated edition of Tom Sawyer," he wrote. He was apparently unaware that Chatto and Windus had not expedited a copyright of the book in Canada, as he notes that he telegraphed a request to the English publisher that the Canadian copyright be assigned to himself — adding, however, "but I suppose it is too late to do any good." Conway replied, sending an assignment of the English copyright to the author, but the author hesitated to make use of it, perhaps due to legal advice that it was useless. Two months later Twain decided to refer the problem back to Chatto and Windus, after Conway had informed the author that Belford Brothers had made no negotiations "of any sort" in respect to *Tom Sawyer*, but noted they often were "in the habit of publishing Chatto and Windus works by agreement." Belford Brothers, however, do not appear to have been too cooperative or worried about their piracy, thus answering a letter from the English publishers: "We should be very sorry to conflict with your interest in any way in Canada. We know Americans are in the habit of taking out copyright in England, but ... we are well advised that it gives no right in Canada." It seems apparent that the Canadians were well aware of the commercial value of *Tom Sawyer*.

After this defeat at the hands of unscrupulous publishers Twain had many choice words to say about pirate publishers over the years whenever he was in the proper frame of mind. On the other hand, there were those moments when he appeared flattered that his works had such importance, or were in such demand that publishers frequently circumvented whatever laws there were in order to issue them. There appears to have been a brisk sale of the pirated edition of *Tom Sawyer*, three printings being issued before the American Publishing Company's edition appeared. Twain convinced himself that these had all but eliminated the Canadian market for sales of his novel. Also, through the mails, together with the sales handled by news agents on the railroad and ship lines, they had reduced the future market for sales of the legal edition of *Tom Sawyer* in the United States, he implied in a letter to Conway.

Whether or not this severely reduced the sales by the American Publishing Company of their more elaborate subscription edition is impossible to determine on the basis of sales records. While Twain told

Conway, "Belford will have sold 100,000 over the frontier and killed my book dead," and later added, "The Canadian 'Tom Sawyer' has actually taken the market from us in every village in the Union," these appear to be among his typical exaggerations. While there was harm done, without doubt, it was probably much less than the author estimated. Since the Canadian edition, published both in paper covers and plum-colored, cloth-covered boards, sold for only 75 cents and $1.00 a copy, respectively, it was sold in most cases to a different clientele than was pursued by the subscription houses. It was a near duplicate of the English edition, having 341 pages and 35 chapters (Belford corrected the numbering of two but not "xii") and no illustrations.* While sales records are sketchy, the Canadian *Tom Sawyer* likely was widely purchased while the American edition was still in preparation.

Appearing also before the American edition was an English language one issued by Bernhard Tauchnitz in Leipzig, Germany, part of the publisher's series, "Collection of British Authors." Baron Tauchnitz, however, had reached Twain through Bret Harte, and when the author replied on September 14, 1876, he expressed his gratification to Tauchnitz for being included in the firm's series and that he was pleased with the courtesy of being notified of the firm's intentions to publish the novel. Tauchnitz was not required by the current laws then to pay any royalties to Twain for this publication of the work in Germany, but according to Alfred Bigelow Paine, he paid the author "of his own will and accord, all that he could afford for this privilege." Twain's letter to Tauchnitz noted that the American edition was still to be delayed "two months," and that he believed there would be no alterations from the English edition, apparently unaware of the minor differences.

The German edition, published in October of 1876, was most likely made from a copy of the book forwarded to Baron Tauchnitz by his London agent. It was a plainly printed volume without illustrations and follows the English edition's text, differing principally only in having 303 printed pages. Although the Tauchnitz edition was not a tranlation, a very early German translation was apparently done by Moritz, published in Leipzig by F.W. Grunow, and the copies in existence carry an 1876 date. If it did appear in accordance with the date it carries, it was indeed a rapidly accomplished translation. Nevertheless, England and Canada were joined by Germany in publishing *The Adventures of Tom Sawyer* in advance of any edition produced in the United States.

The subscription edition, following the common practice, underwent the process of canvassing for several weeks before the first of the elaborate volumes were bound and made ready for delivery to the sales agents. Publication of *Tom Sawyer* in England and Canada apparently did nothing to effect any change in the speed with which Elisha Bliss arranged his sales campaign or printing schedule. The superior appearance of this edition, if production values had as much effect upon the time of publication as some evidence indicates, would be partial

*See Appendix II, page 153.

justification for the delayed publication date. Nothing is easier than to blame Bliss' hesitations rather than Twain's meddling in the publishing process for the problems that the American edition had to overcome. Perhaps, if only privately, both the author and the publisher breathed a sigh of relief when the completed, bound volumes became available to the public on December 8, 1876.

While the "first American edition" was not a true first edition, in many respects it was the most handsome. Work on the American Publishing Company's edition had started over a year before the publication date when True Williams initiated his sketches for the many illustrations, working from the author's original manuscript. It progressed very slowly during the next several months as the artist completed most of his sketches, while Twain attended to the necessary tasks of revision, particularly after his receipt of Howells' suggestions for changes. The galley proofs came early in 1876, while the relationship between Bliss and Twain wavered between calm and storm. Though they clashed frequently over such items as the undetermined, disputed publication date, work moved slowly ahead on the plates for the illustrations while spring turned into summer. The plates appear to have been the source of a large part of the delay, judging from several statements in the author's letters. The final proofs were not available for checking until the months of August and September. These were the proofs of the pages exactly as they would appear in the published volume. Not long after Twain returned the last of these sheets with his approval to Bliss, the steam-powered presses in the Hartford printing plant would have gone to work producing the illustrated pages for the American edition.

Around the middle of November, Bliss began to forward copies of the prospectus to the subscription sales agents to begin taking orders for the novel. The prospectus copy for *Tom Sawyer* contained such highlights of the published story as the midnight graveyard adventure, the mock funeral, the melodramatic trial, and other items selected to please the eyes of the customers. The prospectus contained some generous examples of the novel's illustrations, order blanks to be used by the sales people, and an assortment of samples of the more expensive binding materials in which the book was also to be sold.

Before a month had passed nearly 10,000 copies of the American edition of *Tom Sawyer* were in print. About one out of eight of them had leather bindings of calf, or half morocco; but the majority of the first copies delivered to Bliss and made available to the reading public that month were bound in blue cloth. The blue cloth was highly decorated with a variety of scroll work designs printed in black, with the title on the front cover printed in gold and surrounded by gold stars at the compass points. The spine was only slightly less elaborate in treatment and the back cover comparatively plain, with a central monogram of the American Publishing Company. Although ornate, with a design displaying no particular relevance to the volume's contents, the American first edition stands out from the great numbers of bland, solemn editions in which the work was to appear time and time again (although there have been a few noteworthy exceptions). Some have argued otherwise, such as John T. Winterich, who wrote in his introduction to the 1936 Heritage Club edition of the novel: "Certainly the London edition ... without being a striking example of bookmaking ... excelled the American on esthetic grounds.... The American was ... in an ornate black-and-gold-stamped blue cloth cover (in the cheapest bining) shoddily proofread and as shoddily printed." While there is a portion of truth to these comments, they overlook other facets (such as William's rough illustrations which seem quite fitting to the story, and quaint to today's reader), and they are certainly wrong in regard to the conditions of the English printing (with its faulty numbering of the chapters, and other problems).

Without doubt, whatever esthetic consideration the publisher lavished on the book, most had the purpose of making it appealing to the typical subscription book customer. Similar considerations entered into its oversized physical aspects. The cover measured approximately 22 centimeters high and 17 centimeters deep, this allowing for large pages (of 21½ by 16½ centimeters in size), somewhat irregular dimensions whose purpose were to make the book appear bulky. Also, this size permitted wide margins and lengthy, leisurely lines of type buttressing the profusion of bold illustrations by True Williams sharing over half of the pages. Of the pages, 274 were numbered and the 275th contained the short "Conclusion." All of the earlier printings are reported to have used calendered paper, with bibliographers nothing three stages with slight variations among those issued using the 1876 date of the first edition.

Other printings of *Tom Sawyer* produced by the American Publishing Company, having the same basic appearance, came out with various dates for approximately the next 25 years. Those errors which appeared in the first edition went uncorrected during this period. Copies of the American first edition, though rare, are not extremely rare, having sold over the past decades for prices ranging up to $2,000 for copies in the very best condition, and down to $200 for worn copies. Copies of the English and Canadian editions have frequently sold at somewhat lower prices, whether the result of supply or demand. The largest proportion of copies of the first edition probably remains in private collections; a significant number also are held in public and university libraries across the United States. From its slow start (compared to the rapid initial sales of *Innocents Abroad*, the work which first brought Twain international fame), *The Adventures of Tom Sawyer* has grown in popularity among readers until it presently ranks very high among the American best sellers of all times.

Now, over a hundred years since the novel's first appearance in the English, Canadian, German, and American first editions, it is currently available in a wide variety of editions and bindings. These come in a wide range of prices from the smaller paperback printings to the hard cover, higher priced editions with colored illustrations. Any complete listing of all the many editions of *Tom Sawyer* would be extensive, including necessarily those with the text translated into foreign languages, those containing illustrations by both famed and obscure artists, and the growing numbers prefaced with "introductions" by critics of all calibers. The author of the novel, worrying through the year of 1876 in almost continuous battle with Elisha Bliss and the publisher, could never have had, with the boldest stretching of his imagination, any idea of the success that would finally be accorded his book.

The American Publishing Company's edition was first replaced in 1903 when Harper & Bros. became Twain's official publishers. In 1885, following a growing disenchantment with the American Publishing Company, Mark Twain had founded his own firm (issuing *The Adventures of Huckleberry Finn*, though never any edition of *Tom Sawyer*). Appointed as head of the firm was the husband of his niece, after whom the firm was called C.L. Webster — but, in practice, most major decisions came from Twain. As the firm failed and left the author bankrupt in 1893, he turned over most of his business affairs to Henry H. Rogers, an executive with the Standard Oil Corporation and a friend, Rogers promoting an agreement with Harper & Bros. in the mid-1890's. This led to the signing of an exclusive contract with that firm in October of 1903 for publishing all his works. Thus, until 1931, when the United States copyright on *Tom Sawyer* expired, most of a variety of editions of *Tom Sawyer* came from Harper.

*Tom Sawyer* appeared also during that time in the form of separate editions, and as part of several "collected works" of the author, all authorized by Harper & Bros. but published under such imprints as Collier, Gosset & Dunlap, and the Modern Library. With the approach of the centennial year of Mark Twain's birth, and the expired copyright, at least ten new editions of the work were issued under other imprints.

There have been only a few editions published from 1931 on that deserve special recognition, several of them because of supplementary material or useful introductions, and others because of their famed illustrators. Following earlier editions using introductions by Dr. Percy Boynton (Harper, 1910) and Albert Biglow Paine with Booth Tarkington (Gabriel Wells, v. VIII, *The Works of Mark Twain*, 1922), editions to be singled out are those with introductions by Bertha Evans Ward (Ginn, 1931); Christopher Morley (Winston, 1931); John T. Winterich (Heritage Club, 1936); Bernard DeVoto (Limited Editions Club, 1939); George P. Elliott (Signet, 1959, a slightly revised edition of the text); Clara Clemens, the author's daughter (Pratt & Mink, an edition combined with *Huckleberry Finn*, 1960); Clifton Fadiman (Macmillan, 1962); Diana Trilling (Collier Books, 1962); and Walter Blair (Houghton Mifflin, 1962). Unlisted are a quantity using standard material.

Among the illustrated editions that can be singled out, surpassing in quality, if not in quantity and uniqueness, the rough sketches of True Williams, is the 1936 Heritage Club edition illustrated with the paintings of Norman Rockwell. Noted for his realism, Rockwell went to Hannibal, Missouri, for a firsthand look at the author's hometown, as is evidenced by certain features in several of the paintings. Done in his typical *Saturday Evening Post* cover style, with the regular touches of humor and pathos, his depiction of the characters may leave some purists unsatisfied; but these illustrations stand apart in their realistic approach, and one, that of Tom whitewashing the fence, was used on a United States commemorative postage stamp in 1976. Thomas Hart Benton's work, done for the Limited Editions Club publication of *Tom Sawyer* in 1939, also deserves notice. In all, more than 36 illustrators are known to have applied their diversified talents in depicting the events and leading characters of the novel. Their work was not made easy by the author's sparse descriptions of many of those characters. Thus, the varieties of "Tom Sawyers" are endless, differing in age, size, and dress — some of the artists displaying excellent talent, with the majority tending to be more idealistic than realistic in their concepts. Though the efforts of most of these illustrators have produced pictures whose quality appears to surpass the black and white sketches of True Williams on the basis of technique, none approach in number the 161 items in the first American edition, those chosen by Elisha Bliss from a reported near 200 drawings made by the first illustrator.

Even as illustrators, no matter what their technical proficiency, miss something of the author's original intent when translating the material into their media, so do those whose task it is to translate the author's words and sentences from the original into a foreign language. While some translations seem to succeed sufficiently well to impress millions of readers, those translations that truly reflect or match the original work are indeed rarities. It would seem in the case of Twain, especially in those works where he has given extra attention to the faithful rendering of regional speech, successful translations would be nearly impossible. Even many of the human relationships and life situations he wove into his writings have elements of uniqueness that would offer the faithful translator major problems and tests of skill. Nevertheless, *Tom Sawyer* and others of Twain's writings have been frequently translated for many years, and while it is impossible to judge the results objectively, his popularity in foreign places is equal to, if not greater than, nearly any other American author's.

*The Adventures of Tom Sawyer* has been translated into 33 foreign languages, and possibly into more, this in spite of the proliferation of Americanisms scattered throughout its text. Since appearing in German very near the date of its first publication, and a little later in French, it has been recreated in such diverse languages as Finnish, Macedonian, and Yiddish, not to mention the more prominent tongues. Collections of various translations are in the Library of Congress, at the Mark Twain Memorial Shrine (Florida, Missouri), and at the Mark Twain Museum in Hannibal, with other translations to be found in various libraries. *The Adventures of Huckleberry Finn* and other works by the author have also been translated into a profusion of languages, but *Tom Sawyer* leads them all. Just what Twain might have expressed in regard to this wide translating of his work might only be guessed, but there should be little doubt he would have been happy, even modestly amazed.

However, Twain had a keen awareness of foreign languages, and managed to teach himself to use, with limited proficiency, both German and French. He always had a special affinity for Germany and the Germanic people, and displayed no record of surprise that his writings were given great attention in the German speaking areas. Translations of his work into German, including the largest number of foreign language translations of *Tom Sawyer*, have been done on a continuing basis. Edgar Hemminghaus in *Mark Twain in Germany* lists at least 17 translations of *Tom Sawyer* into German that were done in the period from 1876 to 1936. An additional dozen perhaps could be added to that total since 1936. Hemminghaus estimated that some 240,000 copies of *Tom Sawyer* were printed and sold in Germany up to 1936, and this figure could have doubled easily since then.

While most other countries have not displayed such enthusiasm for Twain's work as have the Germans, a possible exception might be the interest shown by the Russians. There, the author's popularity has been in vogue during the last 50 years, or during those years following the Russian Revolution. Twain's popularity there expanded quickly during those years, and there is perhaps an interest in that country today, particularly among the young readers, in his characters of Tom Sawyer and Huckleberry Finn, which is surpassed only by the readers of the English speaking world. The people of Russia are granted access only to those works that win the approval of bureaucratic administrators. Some of the popularity might be superficially accounted for, as both Tom and Huck present a "revolutionary" approach to life in their society, but extraordinary popularity of works featuring these two characters, as well as other works by Twain, suggest there is real substance to that popularity.

To be answered only by time is the question of whether or not most future editions will be based more on the original version, or upon a recent expertly revised edition. Published in 1979, a new edition of *The Adventures of Tom Sawyer* has been presented as a part of Volume 4 of *The Works of Mark Twain* (published for the Iowa Center for Textual Studies by the University of California Press). This new version, like other titles in this series that have been issued, is an edited version, prepared from both the manuscripts and important early editions, the editors' purpose being "to establish accurate and critically sound texts." It corrects the errors and inconsistencies of those early editions, but since these are mostly minor items, few of the changes would be significant to the average reader. Most valuable in connection with this edition is the supplemental sections providing an introduction and some 200 pages of other material, including a "Genetic Text" of "Boy's Manuscript," all useful to scholars and to students of the novel. For study purposes, such an edition should prove to be second in importance only to the first editions; however, it will be some time before any evidence is found as to whether it has a noticeable influence on the general audience editions. *Tom Sawyer* became a classic without such help, but editing such as this, carefully done, will not prove a hindrance to its continuing status as a classic.

# 13. The Early Reviews

Mark Twain's first reputation as a writer was made as a humorist. His earliest critics, most performing as book reviewers, almost without exception praised his humor, which became universally expected of him, and were uniformly harsh when it failed to fulfill their expectations. There were only a few who looked upon Twain as a serious writer aiming at literature, and fewer who wrote about his earlier work in a manner indicating they saw anything in it of a serious nature. Actually, few critics saw much of literary importance in his work until after his death and even then a decade passed before their numbers grew appreciably.

By 1876 Twain had gained considerable confidence in himself as a writer — and although it was the year in which he began to write *Huckleberry Finn*, his most analyzed and highly acclaimed novel, his chief aim in producing books was to earn a suitable income. That same year, while he did not openly anticipate any serious criticism of *Tom Sawyer*, he expected it would receive much more popular notice in various publications than proved to be the case. Even then, as Twain was aware, book reviews had a broad influence on how well a book sold. To accomplish this end, he had worked closely with two of his influential friends, William D. Howells and Moncure Conway, both closely connected to the efforts to make *Tom Sawyer* a successful novel. It was most fortunate that he did, for without the published aid given the novel by the work of these two, the book would have gone virtually unnoticed at the time of publication. Unfortunately, however, Howells' review, and one by Conway, appeared prematurely in the American press several months in advance of the American edition.

The review by Howells, although it has many of the appearances of being a "put-up-job," was not totally of that nature and was one of the earliest efforts to mark Twain as a serious literary figure. Howells had written to him on November 21, 1875, "Give me a hint when it's to be out and I'll start the sheep to jumping in the right places." Such a remark has the air of a genteel collusion, and to some extent it was because Howells had every intention of helping his friend. In truth, however, and it becomes more apparent as the details are studied, Howells honestly liked the book. Howells had said, earlier in that same letter, "It's altogether the best boy's story I ever read." While this might be taken as an attempt to flatter the author, there is nothing in this or other remarks to indicate that Howells felt otherwise about the work's qualities. Not only did Howells support the book upon his first reading of the entire manuscript, he thereafter gave it praise whenever he expressed his feelings regarding it. It is also clear that Howells had an

96

exceptionally valuable critical position that he needed to maintain, one he would not have risked by word of mouth, in his correspondence, or particularly in the reviews he wrote regularly for the *Atlantic*, the prestige publication he then edited.

That Twain and Howells were both concerned with the hard business facts involved in commercial publication can not be denied, as the evidence for it is apparent. They had no doubts that a good review at the time of publication would result in the sale of many additional copies of any book. The fact that Howells' *Atlantic* review appeared more than six months before the book's American publication, however, practically destroyed whatever usefulness it would have lent to its success. The review did little or nothing to stimulate other reviews or notices for the book, as the *Atlantic*'s editor had hoped it would. Blame for the mistiming lay upon the author, who had believed he had enough influence over the publisher to dictate a publication date. As it was, when Howells' review appeared, the book was not even scheduled for publication in England until a month later, and more than a half year would have to pass before the American edition was to be issued. The delayed publication date therefor contributed much to the unexpected absence of publicity during the next year, even though Howells' effort was well conceived and carried out.

Howells' review, published in the May 1876 issue of the *Atlantic Monthly*, appeared as a part of his "Recent Literature" comments. In this retrospect it featured general statements and was wholly free of adverse criticism. It was likely presented that way because Howells knew it might well set the tone of other reviews to follow it. While Howells' trained mind and literary experience enabled him to discover several features that many later writers would adhere to in their comments on the book, such as the attention he gave its nostalgic qualities, it is also apparent that Howells did not go much beyond the surface of the novel's contents during his reading of it. A busy editor besieged with a constant stream of manuscripts and books, he could hardly give more than a cursory examination to the proof sheets he was furnished. He primarily limited his praise of the story to its importance as juvenile reading, and was more impressed, as most critics were, with Twain's distinctive brand of humor. Howells' review was evidently rapidly written, for in it he twice incorrectly identifies Tom's cousin, Mary, as a "sister." That he did not give more than cursory attention to *Tom Sawyer* in his regular column is understandable — but, in a sense, it can also be understood as a comment on the book.

Because Howells knew the audience he was principally addressing, and not because he was convinced of any intrinsic adult values to be found in the novel, other than the nostalgic and humorous qualities he saw, his review aimed toward presenting the book as "a wonderful study of the boy-mind." Central to this purpose in his review, Howells comments on the realistic portrayal of Tom Sawyer:

> Mr. Clemens ... has taken the boy of the Southwest for the hero of his

new book, and has presented him with a fidelity to circumstance which loses no charm by being realistic in the highest degree, and which gives incomparably the best picture of life in that region as yet known to fiction.

Howells limits all of his comments to brief, general opinions, without detail, a routine performance with little indication of his intellectual reach.

He began the review by comparing *Tom Sawyer* and Aldrich's *A Bad Boy*, though there is no indication that he knew of anything other than a casual relationship between the two novels. He does continue to emphasize the realism of Tom as a fictional character, stating, "The limitations of his transgressions are nicely and artistically traced." A little later, Howells, while making a point of Tom's being normal in most respects, concludes, "What makes him delightful to the reader is that on the imaginative side he is very much more, and though every boy has wild and fantastic dreams, this boy cannot rest till he has somehow realized them." While Tom receives some of the attention he deserves, Howells overlooks the real potential of Huck Finn, saying,

> The worthless vagabond, Huck Finn, is entirely delightful throughout, and in his promised reform his identity is respected: he will lead a decent life in order that he may one day be thought worthy to become a member of that gang of robbers which Tom is to organize.

Fortunately, by this time Twain had made the vital decision that Huck had a greater potential. Howells does, however, show a great deal more insight, toward the end of his review, when he calls attention to the author's ability to create distinctive characters and his unique talent for a realistic portrayal of village life:

> Many village people and local notables are introduced in well-conceived character; the whole town lives in the reader's sense, with its religiousness, its lawlessness, its droll social distinctions, its civilization qualified by its slave-holding and its traditions of the wilder West which has passed away.

It is regrettable that Howells did not enlarge upon this key statement, whether because of lack of space or time, or because he did not recognize its centrality to the novel.

When Howells' review was published and the book was out, Twain became embarrassed, growing increasingly perturbed with the American Publishing Company as the weeks passed. All this is understandable, for the lack of additional reviews was unfortunate; but, since the publisher's principle objective was that the book be issued and sold as a subscription book, Bliss appeared unperturbed, undoubtedly believing the book's prospects rested more with the efficiency of his salespeople than with the publication of reviews. The fact seems to be that few books published by subscription houses received extensive coverage in the book reviews of journals and newspapers, since only a small percentage of the sales were made through regular book dealers. In England this was not the case. The English edition was intended to be sold as one item among many offered at the numerous bookshops, large and small, throughout the British Empire. It was of more obvious importance there that the book, which did appear according to schedule in England, should be provided with as many good reviews as possible.

The securing of favorable book reviews through the use of persons favoring an author's work and willing to cooperate in a book's promotion probably began far back in the history of book publishing, and continues to exist in instances up until today. Authors have occasionally written favorable reviews themselves to assure good reports. Moncure Conway, working as Twain's agent in England on behalf of *Tom Sawyer*, though he stood to receive financial benefits from the sales of the novel, could apparently think it wise, proper, and not uncommon that he should initiate reviews of the book.

That Conway wrote, though he did not sign, the first review of the English edition, appearing in the London *Examiner*, June 17, 1876, is readily accepted. The certainty of his authorship is based on the fact that a second review of the English edition appeared nine days later in an American newspaper, the Cincinnati *Commercial*, bearing the dateline "London, June 10, 1876" and signed with the initials "M.D.C." There are sufficient resemblances between these two reviews to justify believing that they were written by the same person, and undoubtedly the signer of the second was Moncure D. Conway. Before going to England in 1863, Conway had preached for nearly six years in a Cincinnati church, married a Cincinnati woman, and had written some occasional pieces for the Cincinnati press. Thus, not only one, but two reviews appeared in America months before publication of the American edition.

In the *Examiner* review, Conway first showed that he was one of the few who could look upon Twain as more than a humorist. He wrote, "This newest work of Mark Twain increases the difficulty of assigning that author a literary *habitat*." He proclaims that the title "American humorist" is "too vague a label to attach to a writer" who has demonstrated other commendable qualities. "*Tom Sawyer* carries us to an altogether novel region, and along with these characteristics displays a somewhat puzzling variety of abilities." Quoting extensively from the passage where Injun Joe's body is discovered at the sealed entrance to the cave, Conway writes, "In such writing as this we seem to be reading some classic fable." He does not ignore the author's talent with humor, but notes the serious purpose behind it, explaining, "Indeed, a great deal of Mark Twain's humour consists in the serious—or even at times severe—style in which he narrates his stories and pourtrays his scenes, as one who feels that the universal laws are playing through the very slightest of them." Like Howells, Conway was aware that he was writing his review for an adult audience in particular. "The book will no doubt be a favorite with boys, for whom it must in good part have been intended; but next to boys we should say that it might be most prized by philosophers and poets!" Such a point could have originally derived from discussions with the author some six months earlier, but Conway must have agreed.

Although the novel, several times, indicates that the river which flowed past Tom Sawyer's village was the Mississippi, the author of the English review wrote that the book's events "occur in a St. Petersburg situated on the Missouri river." That this unlikely errors appears not only in the London *Examiner* review, but again in the review published in the Cincinnati *Commercial*, provides almost indusputable evidence that the identity of the anonymous author of the first is also the highly suspected author of the second. While there are as many or more differences between the two reviews as there are similarities, less positive indicators such as the style of both pieces, the makeup of the individual sentences and other coincidental points tend to resolve any remaining doubts.

In writing the second review, to appear half-a-world away from the area served by the London *Examiner*, Conway understood that he was writing for a dissimilar audience. Since he knew both of these audiences rather well, he was aware that he would have to design his approach to the book in different ways for each. For the opening in his second review, he says, "Next week all England will be enjoying a new story by Mark Twain, with a piquant sauce supplied by the novelty of reading it before the Centennial land."

The Cincinnati *Commercial* review is lengthier, allowing Conway to quote more liberally from the text. This also allowed him to discuss more leisurely some aspects of the book and to develop those points that he wished to emphasize. Similar to the first review, in this second he notes of *Tom Sawyer*, "It is, as I think, the most notable work which Mark Twain has yet written, and will signally add to his reputation for variety of powers." While making this point in both reviews, in the case of the second, although Conway indicates that Twain is more than just another humorist, he puts more emphasis on the amount and quality of the humor in the book. He also calls particular attention to Huckleberry Finn, whom he declares "a unique and vigorously drawn character," and follows this by quoting from the text the author's description of Huck at the point of his initial appearance. Conway clearly felt that the *Commercial*'s audience would bear more appreciation for this apparent ruffian than would the *Examiner*'s. He also emphasized that "most of the adventures recorded ... really occurred" and that "Huck Finn is drawn from life."

Once more, in this second review, Conway points out that the book will be read by both "grown up folk" as well as by boys and girls, leaving no doubt that he believes the novel has values for the adult reader.

As was customary at that time, a number of other newspapers

located around the country selected parts of the review to reprint, since any report of another book by Mark Twain had, by then, become a newsworthy item. Learning of these extracts in some manner, Twain was initially mystified about their origin, not having been aware of the review Conway had placed in the Cincinnati *Commercial*, until he happened upon a complete reprinting of the "London Letter" in a Hartford newspaper, a town where interest in Twain and his work was the highest. The length and the laudatory content apparently pleased the author of the novel, and he sent Conway a message of thanks .

Since these reviews, both by Conway and Howells, were principally notices of the book's appearance and because they were written by interested friends of the author, they did not contain adverse criticism, and actually offered little more than a brief suggestion of favorable critical content as opposed to ordinary praise. Most of the statements made by these first two reviewers were general statements given with only slender supportive arguments. Between the two, although Howells would seem to have been the better equipped to understand the book, Conway's reviews, particularly that in the *Examiner*, show him to be more aware of Twain's eventual value as a literary light and of the value of this particular book to his career.

Whatever influence these reviews had on the actual sales of the book would seem minimal, for certainly they failed to encourage other critics to give the book attention. One of the main objectives in writing their reviews was, as Howells had put it, "to start the sheep to jumping." However, the reviews that followed these not only lacked the original enthusiasm, but were fewer in number than had been hoped. The delayed publication of the American edition undoubtedly had some effect upon the sparsity of reviews it received there, but this was not the case in England where *Tom Sawyer* had been published and reviews would have been timely.

The first follow-up review in England appeared in the June 24, 1876, issue of the *Athenaeum*. Its anonymous author remains undisclosed and hardly worth speculation. As an influential literary publication, a good notice in the *Athenaeum* would have provided useful help to the book's early reputation and sales. Unfortunately, the reviewer selected for the task knew of Twain only as a humorist whose writing was found in cheap publications. If the reviewer did know any of Twain's already famed books, minimal evidence was offered, or suggested by the tone of the review. It was only reluctantly granted, that in reading *Tom Sawyer*, the vain reviewer had been "made to laugh; and that ought to be taken as high praise." The author of such a brief review might be forgiven for not understanding a book recently published which would a hundred years later remain only partly understood, but in an overbearing sentence the reviewer makes a puzzling assessment, one that could only have resulted from a hasty or shallow conception:

The humour is not always uproarious, but it is genuine and

sometimes almost pathetic, and it is only now and then that the
heartiness of a laugh is spoilt by one of the pieces of self-consciousness
which are common blots on Mark Twain's other books.

The haughty attitude demonstrated by the reviewer also led to the
finding of fault with the use of "slang words and racy expressions" in
places other than "in the conversations."

A slightly longer and more favorable review appeared next in the
London *Times*, on August 28, 1876. Again the review was unsigned and
its writer remains unknown. More sympathetic to Twain's brand of
humor, this reviewer displayed some understanding of the story's events
and discovered the characters to be both entertaining and interesting.
But only a few points are given recognition in the review, the particular
genius of Twain exhibited by his handling of the material of his "native
village," Tom's apparent acquaintance with "literature of an eccentric
kind," and the book's basic tone of drollery. In making a closing sum-
mation of the novel, however, the reviewer supplies only a superficial
observation of the true values later critics would discover in the work:

> The drollery is often grotesque and extravagant, and there is at
> least as much in the queer Americanizing of the language as in the
> ideas it expresses. Practical people who pride themselves on strong
> common sense will have no patience with such vulgar trifling. But
> those who are alive to the pleasure of relaxing from serious thought
> and grave occupation will catch themselves smiling over every page
> and exploding outright over some of the choicer passages.

Obviously, these unknown critics both had concluded before they
began to read *Tom Sawyer* that Twain's one valuable trait was as a
writer of humor. They might have redeemed the narrowness of their
reviews if they had expanded on what they only briefly hinted — that the
work offered more than humor.

The first review of note which followed the issuance of the
American Publishing Company's subscription edition in December of
1876 appeared in the *New York Times* on January 13, 1877. It again was
an unsigned review, apparently done by the sort of reviewer who works
under the pressure of reading many items and is therefore required to
read hurriedly and give only general impressions. In this review, as
much or more space is allotted to a personal philosophy of books for
children as is given to the book at hand. However, it is wisely noted:
"...a truly clever child's book is one in which both man and boy can find
pleasure. No child's book can be perfectly acceptable otherwise."

Though the *Times* review found *Tom Sawyer* to be "amusing," a
sensitivity to so-called realism is perceived in these remarks:

> Since association is everything, it is not desirable that in real life we
> should familiarize our children with those of their age who are law-
> less or dare devils. Granting that the natural is true, and the true is

best, and that we may describe things as they are for adult readers, it is proper that we should discriminate a great deal more as to the choice of subjects in books intended for children.

Twain, as a moralist, however, saw things differently, cleverly suggesting through *Tom Sawyer*, a point the *Times* reviewer missed, that those moral standards conceived for children should also apply to the adult world as well. The reviewer indicated great concern for the wisdom of an author who wrote of "revenge" and "slitting women's ears" and who created such an aura of truth about a villain as Injun Joe, insisting that it "throws an unnecessarily sinister tinge over the story."

The reviewer did, if only briefly, recognize in the book and in Mark Twain the beginnings of craftsmanship, noting, "If Mr. Clemens has been wanting in continuity in his longer sketches, and that sustained inventive power necessary in dovetailing incidents, Tom, as a story, though slightly disjointed, has this defect less apparent." The reviewer was able to recognize at least that as "a humorist, Mr. Clemens has a great deal of fun in him, of the true American kind, which crops out all over the book." While admitting, "We like, then, the true boyish fun of Tom and Huck, and have a foible for the mischief these children engage in," Tom was earlier described as "a preternaturally precocious urchin." Yet, it is in the assessment of Huckleberry Finn that the reviewer shows the best judgment: "one admirable character in the book, and touched with the hand of a master, is that of Huckleberry Finn. There is a reality about this boy which is striking."

Perhaps this review resulted in *Tom Sawyer*'s being denied a few young readers. Sales did not come up to Twain's initial high expectations. In *Mark Twain and Elisha Bliss*, Hamlin Hill reports that only a disappointing 13,319 copies of *Tom Sawyer*'s American edition had sold during the first two months it was available. And, although as Hill added, the book sold only 35,000 copies by 1885, that can hardly be termed unsuccessful. At least it continued to be available, to sell, and especially to gain the admiration of readers, young and old alike. Although *Tom Sawyer* was widely ignored by reviewers and critics, and Twain himself was most frequently looked upon as a mere, though talented, humorist, it was the author's books themselves that won him his steadily growing acclaim. Roger Asselineau in *The Literary Reputation of Mark Twain from 1910 to 1950* has noted:

> His books won popular acclaim, the intelligent reading public regarding him as a literary artist of the first rank, but for at least thirty-five years most reviewers during his lifetime rejected him altogether.

It was not an easily won success, but with books like *Tom Sawyer* and *Huckleberry Finn* bearing the marks of genius, what the reviewers thought and wrote made no difference. Real classics have a way of making themselves known.

# 14. The Growth of Criticism

During the last half of his life, Mark Twain enjoyed great popularity, at home and abroad. He was continually sought after by publishers of books and magazines. Wherever he went, reporters invariably appeared seeking an interview, or at the least a few lines to quote in a news story. As a lecturer, touring the world, he managed to pay off an enormous debt which had almost forced him to declare bankruptcy. This aura of popularity was as much a hindrance to Twain as if it were a curse, for although he desired the benefits it brought, as time went on he could not escape from the label of humorist. Critics continued to treat his work as humor and noticed, only on rare occasions, the values it contained. Sensitive to this situation, he continually tried harder to uncover the deeper thoughts that troubled him, though a substantial part of that work was disregarded until after his death. The public, then and now, has continued to demand his humor and to love him for it.

During his long years, oscillating between failure and success, casting more manuscripts aside than he finished, he sought more and more to make his writing carry a message, but even many of his closest friends had only limited insight to his more serious values. Not even *Huckleberry Finn*, a masterpiece universally declared his finest work, brought him any of the serious notice he desired as a writer. While he drew overwhelming popular acclaim, even among a number of the important critics of his day, he received only a smattering of scholarly attention.

Nothing occurred to show that this lack of academic reception might ever change until the publication of an article in the *Overland Monthly* of April 1898. On this occasion, which generated little attention at the time, Theodore de Laguna, a graduate student at the University of California, Berkeley, included some unusual and telling remarks in his essay entitled "Mark Twain as a Prospective Classic." None had considered this a real possibility up to this point, for as de Laguna wrote, Twain "has been willing to be popular," and his "most enthusiastic admirers have been farthest from suspecting in him the elements of greatness." Searching for a reason for the author's situation, de Laguna analyzes it in the following words:

> In a language as old as ours, it is inevitable that the diction and idiom of culture should be widely differentiated from common speech and serenely elevated above its coarseness and vulgarity. But Mark Twain has persisted in his attachment to his mother tongue. It is hard for a college-bred man to forgive him.

After observing that "Twain very evidently supposes that his humor degrades neither himself, nor his readers, nor, necessarily, the subject of his discourse," de Laguna states that there is more to the author and his art than humor, that his "wood pictures" are among "the most sublime or beautiful natural descriptions in our literature." He notes that his favorite descriptive passage is one from *Tom Sawyer* in which the hero beheld "the dawning of his first day of freedom." While de Laguna admits to the disjointedness of Twain's narratives as opposed to his skill with "the briefest form of narrative, the anecdote," he also proclaims Twain "a story teller; let him be judged as such." As to *Tom Sawyer*, this scholar ranks it with *Aladdin*, "almost any one of Chaucer's tales," and *Robinson Crusoe*.

Performing with candor and foresight unusual for a critic of that day, de Laguna argues that "Twain's style is of infinite import. Aesthetically it has been seriously undervalued." In Twain's writings he could see a "quality of 'harmony',," which he notes rhetoricians "once held to be the rare and distinguishing charm of the highest literary genius."

Directing his attention to *Tom Sawyer*, de Laguna states that with critics the book "met with some strange misappreciation." (Earlier in his essay he had noted that *Tom Sawyer* "is almost beyond criticism" because of its loose construction.) He believes the lack of critical appreciation was illustrated by their failure to evaluate the power of such incidents as that in the cave, while they blindly concentrated on the book's incidental humor.

> When that young scamp is brought face to face with darkness, loneliness, horror, agony, and death, with a timid, helpless child clinging to him alone for comfort in her utter despair, — his thoughtfulness, his patient kindness, his boyish soul's long-suffering endurance, must — it would seem — suffice to distinguish him from "the thousands which anyone familiar with the commercial industry of writing books for boys can name only too readily!"

With insight that might today be taken for granted, de Laguna writes, "Huck is evidently the prose, as Tom is the poetry of Mark Twain's younger self...."

Earlier he writes, "It has been wisely said that no mere humorist can be great, even as a humorist; but it seems hard to believe that the intended victim of the aphorism was Mark Twain." De Laguna senses that the academic world in 1898 was becoming aware of Twain's contributions to literature, yet this essay was an isolated opinion of the author, and especially of *Tom Sawyer*, raising the novel to a level above that of the common boy's book, and certainly above books crowded with humor, but nothing else.

Although by the end of the 19th century, Twain had written and published enough of his work to deserve a change in his stature as America's leading humorist, the change was only to slowly come.

William D. Howells, his longtime friend, in an essay, "Mark Twain: An Inquiry" (published in the *North American Review*, February 1901), made a spirited argument for a reversal of the rejection the author met with as a result of his success with humor. Perhaps Howells was upset by a now little known journalist who that same year had written for the *Bookman*, "Mark Twain is first and last and all the time, so far as he is anything, a humourist and nothing more." Yet another writer, no doubt directly meeting the challenge of that statement, wrote for the *Book Buyer* a short essay titled, "Mark Twain: More Than Humorist." But, even with the awarding of an honorary degree to Twain in 1908 by Oxford University in England, an award given with as much attention to the author's humor as to his serious literary achievements, his status changed but little.

While little attention was being given the author as a writer of works having a literary value, almost none at all was given *Tom Sawyer* except as a work to be valued for its nostalgia of a disappearing past, or as a boy's adventure book. William Lyon Phelps, one of the few critics seeing the need to question the low esteem given Twain's writings in text books on American literature, was also among the earliest to recognize that *Tom Sawyer* was a significant work. He held an opinion, much like the earlier *New York Times* reviewers, that for a work to have status as a classic it must appeal to readers of all ages — declaring *Tom Sawyer* to be

> one of those books — of which *The Pilgrim's Progress*, *Gulliver's Travels*, and *Robinson Crusoe* are supreme examples — that are read at different periods of one's life from different points of view; so that it is not easy to say when one enjoys them the most — before one understands their real significance or after.

Elsewhere, in the chapter, "Mark Twain," from *Essays on Modern Novelists* (Macmillan, 1910), Phelps says, "Although Mark Twain has the great qualities of the true humorist ... he is much more than a humorist." While Phelps seemed to be aware of the greatness of both *Tom Sawyer* and *Huckleberry Finn*, speaking highly of the art he found in them, he never expanded his remarks into a full treatment of these works.

Perhaps Twain's relatively modest stature at this time was not totally the fault of the critics, for the author had himself done much to create the image by which he was universally recognized. His family and his friends had been encouraged to support that public image and they chose to do so. Albert Bigelow Paine, his biographer, being almost unique in the access he had to Twain during the author's final decade, to his opinions and to his papers, stuck closely to the popular image in nearly all that he revealed in his massive biography, except for some scattered vague hints. Paine's comments relevant to *Tom Sawyer* took their tone, as did most of the comments by Twain himself, from the general opinions formed early about the novel, which had all but crystalized.

Strange as it may seem initially, some of the most serious consideration allotted Twain at this point came out of Germany. Charles Alphonso Smith, an American professor on leave from the University of Virginia to conduct a seminar with lectures on American literature at Berlin University during 1910 and 1911, included an enlightening one on Twain. "Mark Twain und der amerikanische Humor" was collected in *Die amerikanische Literatur* in 1912. Since this work has apparently never been translated into English, it has influenced only minutely the study of Mark Twain here, one of the few places it received attention useful to other than readers of German being in Edgar H. Hemminghaus' *Mark Twain in Germany* (Columbia, 1939).

In his lecture, Smith found in Twain's work a tendency towards contrasts. "Among the most dominant factors that served to develop that tendency were the period and place of his birth," Smith is quoted by Hemminghaus as saying. Smith said this provided Mark Twain with a background giving him contact with contrasts in persons, social classes, ideas and institutions of a variety not available to many authors. Smith found it used prominently in *The Adventures of Tom Sawyer*, particularly in the contrast between Tom the romantic and Huck the realist. Contrast served in nearly all of the author's work, Smith contended, down to the last. Twain's humor served especially to make the contrasts more vivid, and Smith noted that humor's chief purpose in the works was not as mere entertainment, but rather criticism, often appearing exaggerated humor as he attempted to express that which could not be expressed in a simple fashion.

Signs of an improvement in criticism on Mark Twain, and especially *Tom Sawyer*, continued to be rare during the decade from 1910 to 1920. In that latter year, *The Ordeal of Mark Twain* by Van Wyck Brooks was published, signalling a beginning to serious study of the author's life and work. Brooks gave only limited attention to *Tom Sawyer*, perhaps thinking of it when he wrote, "We find Mark Twain in perpetual revolt against all those institutions for which his mother stood." Brooks marshalled pages of argument to show that Mark Twain, although talented as an artist, had allowed his family and his public to censure his genius and to stifle his rebellious art. Such a picture of the writer's life and career, differing with the common assessment, led more American critics to take a closer look and to reevaluate the author and his writings.

As the stream of criticism began to branch out following the publication of Brooks' views, *Tom Sawyer* received only limited attention, mostly receiving comment in conjunction with *Huckleberry Finn*, or the writings of Mark Twain in general. Brander Matthews, in *The Tocsin of Revolt and Other Essays* (Scribners, 1922), having had personal contacts with the author, used a short section of this book to throw new light on the composition of *Tom Sawyer*, reporting that Twain once explained how he had written certain items first out of his memories, then rewrote and revised the material, waiting at times for inspiration to strike again.

A more serious contribution to criticism of *Tom Sawyer* was supplied by Olin Harris Moore in his essay "Mark Twain and Don Quixote" (*Publications of the Modern Language Association*, 1922), where he pointed out the visible influence that Cervantes had on the author of *Tom Sawyer*. He noted "that there is a striking parallel between the plot of *Don Quixote*, on the one hand, and of *Tom Sawyer* and *Huckleberry Finn* on the other," designating a number of similarities. While Moore may have overemphasized the influence of a single author, the point he made is of continuing use to *Tom Sawyer* criticism.

With an essay, "Mark Twain in Iowa" (*Iowa Journal of History and Politics*, 1929), Fred Lorch contributed brief facts relevant to the history of *Tom Sawyer*, among the many contributions he was to make toward criticism of the author. Soon after the above, works by Bernard DeVoto and Minnie M. Brashear appeared providing additional research of benefit to future students of *Tom Sawyer* and its creator. DeVoto, disturbed by Paine's attempts to cut off debate about Twain by refusing others access to the author's papers and by Brooks' use of Twain as an example of a frustrated American artist, wrote *Mark Twain's America* (Little Brown, 1932), a work in which he objected strongly to Brooks' thesis. DeVoto felt that Brooks had overlooked certain facts in Twain's background and success as a "frontier humorist." DeVoto wrote: "He took the humorous anecdote, combined it with autobiographical reminiscence, and so achieved the narrative form best adapted to his mind." He also noted that Twain "could not for long discipline his thinking or his writing." Though DeVoto wrote more as a historian than as a critic, the materials of his research stimulated increased attention to the author.

Research as well as criticism that contributed much to Twain scholarship and has led to a better understanding of *The Adventures of Tom Sawyer* was provided by Minnie Brashear in *Mark Twain: Son of Missouri* (University of North Carolina Press, 1934). Asking the question, "Given so arresting a mind and personality, how is it to be accounted for?" Brashear found the answer in his birthplace: "As a matter of fact, it is doubtful whether, anywhere in America, there could have been found in the forties and fifties [of the 19th century] a small section of country more favorable for his start in life than northeast Missouri." Apparently reflecting on the German essay by Charles Alphonso Smith (which she lists in her bibliography, she being one of the few critics to pay attention to that essay), she looks carefully at Twain's birthplace, his childhood home and his "college" attended as a pilot on the Mississippi — finding not the barren background that others saw, but one intellectually alive and stimulating for the education of an author.

Brashear calls attention to the people, the activities, the institutions, and the culture of the area where he grew into maturity, supporting her argument further with a listing of all the possibilities open to young Clemens for reading books and other materials. Some of her suggestions regarding his reading can be easily confirmed, others only assumed, but she notes that the basic influences in his work belong to the

Bible, Shakespeare, Cervantes, and certain 18th century authors and philosophers. She notes that while his reading provided valuable tools and molded his style, the subject and content of his important work came more definitely from the fortunate place and time of his birth. *The Adventures of Tom Sawyer* and *The Adventures of Huckleberry Finn*, she notes in particular, had their unique origins in that background.

Another critic who has contributed to the understanding of the success of *Tom Sawyer* by investigations of its origins is Walter Blair. In his book *Native American Humor (1800–1900)* (American Book Co., 1937) he points out B.P. Schillaber's apparently early and continuing influence on characters and situations in Twain's fiction. Later, in 1939, Blair published one of the more important essays, "On the Structure of Tom Sawyer" (*Modern Philology*). Following a close study of both the book and its manuscript, Blair demonstrated that the novel, contrary to many critics' views, has a distinctive pattern of development, a form imposed upon the material to provide for a maturing of its hero Tom. Although this essay does not demolish all of the arguments to the contrary, it has had the effect of lifting the book to a higher plane of criticism.

Likewise, serious views toward *Tom Sawyer* were stimulated by — and profited from — the publication of the "Boy's Manuscript." This predecessor of *Tom Sawyer* was first published as a part of the Limited Editions Club's edition of *Tom Sawyer* (1939), and later became a part of Bernard DeVoto's *Mark Twain at Work* (Harvard University Press, 1942). Following many years of criticising Paine and Brooks, DeVoto found himself appointed to the position of custodian of the Mark Twain Papers in 1938. Among the things he accomplished in that position was the recognition and publication of this long neglected, first attempt by Twain to use material from his Hannibal boyhood in an extended sketch. DeVoto noted in an accompanying essay that the "Boy's Manuscript" is "crude and trivial, false in sentiment, clumsily farcial, an experiment in burlesque with all of its standards mixed." However, he thought it important because it "prophesies not *Tom Sawyer* only but *Huckleberry Finn* as well...." DeVoto's essay gives some extended attention to the composition of *Tom Sawyer*, touching some of the basic facts regarding the work's origins. He examines Twain's "episodic method of composition," which, he explains, undoubtedly "shows in the book's indifference to minutiae." Loosely as the book appears to be constructed, DeVoto contends, "Structurally *Tom Sawyer* is a better job than most of Mark's fiction." He notes the story's illusion of realism, exclaiming, "What is asserted of it is all memorably true but much has been left out." In a sense, DeVoto says, "the book became a pastoral poem, an idyll of an America that had already vanished when it was written...."

DeVoto also points out a factor that had been either overlooked or avoided by critics: "The book's enchantment is so strong that it beguiles one into forgetting how much of the spell issues from dread and horror." *Tom Sawyer*, he claims, "transcends realism, transcends its narrative, transcends its character and becomes mythology.' Thus DeVoto lifts it to a classic, though many of his comments remain too general in nature.

Literary histories, like Carl Van Doren's *The American Novel, 1789–1939*, have since midcentury given greater attention to Twain and included more discussion of *Tom Sawyer*. Other works devoted exclusively to Twain began to appear, taking increased notice of *Tom Sawyer* as a serious subject. An essay by Ray B. West, Jr., "Mark Twain's Idyl of Frontier America" (*University of Kansas City Review*, 1948–49), treated aspects of the development of Twain's literary art, seeing many of its strengths arising from the author's upbringing in a frontier locale. West adds his personal opinion to those finding evidence of form in the novel:

> The structure achieved in *Tom Sawyer* is not an integration of action with theme and character, but is rather that of the conventional plotted story, an artificially contrived structure which gives the impression of form without achieving it.

Another essay, one analyzing a central problem of the book, is "Splendid Days and Fearsome Nights," written by Svend Peterson and published in 1949 (*Mark Twain Quarterly*). It follows the chronology of events in *Tom Sawyer*. Peterson points out some of the disturbing details regarding the passage of time in the novel, offering explanations that help to answer some questions arising from the overburdened time scheme which the author imposed upon his story.

There is little doubt that Twain had by 1950 become a subject of major effort among literary critics and scholars. In that year Gladys Carmen Bellamy published *Mark Twain as a Literary Artist* (University of Oklahoma Press). Her study touches many of the pros and cons of the author's status, making isolated references to *Tom Sawyer*. She noted that while *Tom Sawyer* was "inartistic in its minor effects — in the momentary impact of its melodramatic scenes, for instance — the book is ultimately satisfying because it has the artistic tension between life forces, the equilibrium necessary for art." She gives prominence to the opinions of Walter Blair, noting their value, while pointing out some of the deficiencies in the opinions of Bernard DeVoto, ending her discussion of the book by saying, "The book has the permanency of a beautiful fairy tale."

Allowing the novel special attention, but seeing it almost wholly in terms of its symbolic content, thought to be important to its understanding, Kenneth S. Lynn in his book *Mark Twain and Southwestern Humor* (Little, Brown, 1958) presents an analysis of the work's adult appeal. Lynn's observations of the use of extensive symbolism in Twain's writings exceed most previous estimates of the author's literary abilities. While there appears to have been ample opportunities for Twain to have had contact through his reading with many of the symbolic themes Lynn claims are presented in his writings, most critics have not considered *Tom Sawyer* as growing out of the intellectual stimulations of literature as much as out of his Hannibal childhood experiences. Lynn's work, however, does help the student to understand better that *The Ad-*

*ventures of Tom Sawyer*, while it uses a large amount of autobiographical material, is not in any strict sense an autobiographical novel, and
that Twain, though he gives in this novel an air of reality, completely
distorts and disguises the true facts as needed to confirm with the needs
of his artistic purposes.

A variety of critical essays, though not all of equal importance, appeared during the decade of the 1950's, some advancing new opinions,
others reworking old opinions. Among the more unusual was "Sawyer et
al. v. Administrator of Injun Joe," by Elmer M. Million (*Missouri Law
Quarterly*, 1951), a legal interpretation of the rightful title to the
treasure found by Tom and Huck in the cave. In the *Mark Twain Quarterly* (1952), George Santayana, writing "Tom Sawyer and Don
Quixote," offered more regarding the influence of Cervantes on the
author of the novel. Louis Leary's "Tom and Huck: Innocence on Trial"
(*Virginia Quarterly Review*, 1954) undertook a thorough analysis of the
novel that applies some fresh thought to its values for mature readers. A
discussion of some of the possibilities surrounding the sources of the
name of the novel's hero is presented in "On the Naming of Tom
Sawyer," by William G. Barrett (*Psychoanalytic Quarterly*, 1954).
Barry Marks in "Mark Twain's Hymn of Praise" (*The English Journal*,
1959) sought to examine some of the philosophical flavor of the novel.
Published as an Afterword at the back of the 1959 Signet Classic edition of
*Tom Sawyer*, George P. Elliott's short essay, titled "Vacation in
Boyhood," sees the novel as a nonserious work, an excursion into
boyhood which though it is unpretentious is still praiseworthy, not for its
correctness and form but for its relief from formalities; Elliott wrote that
the book came from "the hands of a master." This same decade produced
several books that touch in part on *Tom Sawyer*, some with instances of
valuable insight, with D.M. McKeithan's *Court Trials in Mark Twain
and Other Essays* (Martinus Nijhoff, 1958) worthy of special mention for
its treatment of the murder trial in a chapter designated "The Trial of
Muff Potter in *Tom Sawyer*."

Since 1960, criticism applied to *Tom Sawyer* has been made the
subject of dozens of essays and a part of many books treating Twain,
allowing only the most innovative to be noted here. High on any listing
would be Walter Blair's *Mark Twain and Huck Finn* (University of
California, 1960), a book which, although it is a study of *Huckleberry
Finn* in essence, also provides useful attention to *Tom Sawyer* in both
Chapter 4 of the volume and in background material. What Blair has
done here essentially supplements his earlier essay and is especially
valuable in its treatment of the relationship of *Tom Sawyer* to its sequel.
In a summary fashion Blair brings together what he considers all the
worthwhile information and theses concerning the novel and its composition, adding bits of his original research. He voices a conclusion that
"Literary influences thus shaped both incidents and the over-all pattern
of *Tom Sawyer*."

Another volume giving important attention to *Tom Sawyer* is
Franklin R. Rogers' *Mark Twain's Burlesque Patterns* (Southern

Methodist University Press, 1960). Rogers, in accord with his central thesis, emphasizes the many uses of burlesque techniques in the novel, stressing their importance to the general structure of the book. He takes note of Twain's earlier experiments with burlesque, including the "Boy's Manuscript," and indicates how these influenced the completed novel, paying particular attention to the tendency of the author's burlesquing efforts to echo those in Dickens' *David Copperfield*. Rogers' opinions, while pointing out that in the early stages of his career Twain was a deliberate humorist, considers the author no less important as an accomplished artist, and notes that *Tom Sawyer* is "one of Twain's most carefully constructed novels."

Published in 1961, *The Innocent Eye: Childhood in Mark Twain's Imagination* by Albert E. Stone, Jr. (Yale University Press) is another general work of criticism about Twain's writings, but it has much to say about *Tom Sawyer*. Stone presents a view that although the book was finally directed toward juvenile readers, it lost little of the content that made it a novel written originally for adults. Stone places a high value on Twain's use of interacting and balancing themes, noting: "What begins as a 'play adventure' for boys in the graveyard mushrooms into melodrama and turns, finally, into a moral crisis." Stone contends that the novel is generally well constructed, but notes that Twain's disillusionment with the book was his

> realization that boyhood as he recalled and recreated it in *Tom Sawyer* was not such a convenient escape from controversial topics as he had hoped, instead childhood was deceptively nostalgic and appealing, an ambiguous realm filled with unexpected emotional and literary pitfalls.

Some of Stone's opinions are convenient to use as general evaluations of the novel, for they show a penetrating analysis of the book's structure, adding fresh insight into Twain's aims and methods; they cannot, however, be accepted as conclusive descriptions.

Also published in 1961, Frank Baldanza's general volume, *Mark Twain: An Introduction and Interpretation* (Barnes & Noble), provides a concise evaluation of *Tom Sawyer*, section by section, and a fresh interpretation of parts. Baldanza's discussion of the book in terms of various "guilt cycles," when applied to the high points of the novel, furnishes an interesting analysis of the author's themes and intentions. While it is chiefly intended as introductory material for students, its reference to special items, such as the contrast between Tom and Huck as "a dichotomy that must represent two very profound aspects of Clemens' own nature," make it a useful work of criticism.

An essay written by Hamlin Hill, "The Composition and the Structure of Tom Sawyer" (*American Literature*), also a highlight of 1961, both summarizes previous opinions and adds considerable original research gathered from an examination of the original manuscript. Some of this became a part of his volume, *Mark Twain and Elisha Bliss*

(University of Missouri, 1964), covering the problems of Twain with his first publishers and therefore adding to our knowledge of *Tom Sawyer's* progress from manuscript to published volume.

A valuable examination of Twain's art and writing methods appears in *Mark Twain: The Development of a Writer* (Harvard University Press, 1962) by Henry Nash Smith. Smith devotes approximately ten pages to a discussion of the problems concerned with *Tom Sawyer*. His criticisms are at times strong, but balanced with praise for Twain's use of exceptional, clear, concise prose. Smith, observing the structural problems of the novel, notes that while Twain sought solutions, he could never escape the limitations imposed by the material, the burlesque love story and the Bad Boy, Good Boy theme. As both literary editor of the Mark Twain Estate and coeditor of the useful *Mark Twain–Howells Letters* (Harvard University Press, 1961), Smith's comments are important and deserve the attention of all.

*Mark Twain: Jackleg Novelist* by Robert Wiggins (University of Washington Press, 1964) uses the term "jackleg" to describe Mark Twain as an improvisor rather than as a systematic writer of novels. Wiggins devoted a chapter to *Tom Sawyer* in which he observed that the author created the work in a simple, oral style, using exaggerated spellings sparingly and relying on idiom and syntax for the desired effects. William C. Spengemann, in *Mark Twain and the Backwoods Angel* (Kent State University Press) published in 1966, felt the author was uncertain as to what the chief theme of *Tom Sawyer* was to be, an "adult's amused view of childhood," an attempt "to recreate his own boyhood ... to portray innocence," or "to show that a bad boy could succeed as well as the good boys," and thus found the work to be weakly constructed. Spengemann, like Wiggins, however, sees the book as not a complete failure if only because Twain was able to "salvage a hero, a point of view, and a setting" for his more noted *Huckleberry Finn*. Also, making use of another symbolic theme from literature to examine Twain's work, Robert Regan, in *Unpromising Heroes: Mark Twain and His Characters* (University of California Press, 1966), gives some particular attention to *Tom Sawyer*. Regan writes: "That *The Adventures of Tom Sawyer* is a success story squarely situated in the Unpromising Hero tradition is obvious." While giving much attention to the technical and symbolic aspects in his criticism, Regan also proclaims, "The novel is neither so pretentious nor so successful as to deserve being judged by the most demanding critical canons."

Another work, published in 1966, *Mark Twain: The Fate of Humor* by James M. Cox (Princeton University Press), furnishes the novel an analysis almost exclusively of Twain's use of dramatic terms and literary techniques. Some of Cox's observations are unique, but most are too abstract for any practical application, though some furnish a degree of understanding why the book succeeds even while it appears on the surface to be loosely composed.

Louis D. Rubin, Jr., in his essay "Tom Sawyer and the Use of Novels," published as part of *The Curious Death of the Novel* (Louisiana

State University Press, 1967), praises *Tom Sawyer* for its rich insight into "what American life means":

> Not the repudiation of success and practicality, but the achievement of it. Tom has succeeded. He has changed his world. He is rich, and famous, and heroic. He would not have it differently, and neither would his creator. Yet along with it there is the sense of something impractical and spiritual lost in the doing.

Focusing on what happens to Tom and his pals and what this means for us, Rubin asks, and answers, "What, in short, is this novel about *as a novel?* One of Rubin's conclusions is that "while the novel lasts, Tom Sawyer holds on to life on a child's terms, and forces the community to accept it." Jay Martin, in *Harvests of Change, American Literature, 1856–1914* (Prentice-Hall, 1967), while allotting only a few pages to *Tom Sawyer*, observes that in writing the book "Twain could not have failed to recognize how much this fable was a parable accurately summarizing his own career. Although astonishingly successful as a writer, he resisted the society that rewarded him."

During the 1960's more was written about Twain and his writings than had ever been written about him in any decade before, possibly more than will ever be written during a similar period in the future. Among the books and especially essays of that decade, many contribute bits and pieces of minor information useful to the critic and student of *Tom Sawyer*. In the present work there is room to cite only those items directed especially at that novel.

A broad look at the book, "Setting and Theme in *Tom Sawyer*" by William B. Dillingham, was published in the *Mark Twain Journal*, 1964. Diana Trilling presented a sociological–psychological view of the novel, in "Tom Sawyer, Delinquent," included in her volume *Claremont Essays* (Harcourt, Brace & World, 1964). John Halverson suggests that Chaucer's influence is seen in Chapter 8 of the novel, this in "Patristic Exegesis: A Medieval *Tom Sawyer*" (*College English*, 1965). "Parallel Scenes in *Tom Sawyer* and *Huck Finn*" (*The CEA Critic*, 1967), by William R. Manierre, takes a look at Twain's habit of rehearsals. In Robert Tracy's "Myth and Reality in *The Adventures of Tom Sawyer*" (*Southern Review*, 1968), a theory of the book's possible symbolic content is advanced. An essay exploring similarities to Cooper is presented in "Huckleberry Bumpo: A Comparison of *Tom Sawyer* and *The Pioneers*" (*Mark Twain Journal*, 1968), written by Sacvan Bercovitch. Still another essay touching on some of the possible literary themes of the story is given by L. Moffitt Cecil in "Tom Sawyer: Missouri Robin Hood" (*Western American Literature*, 1969). Although these and other items helped expand the critical writing provided *Tom Sawyer*, the corpus remained small in comparison to that surrounding *Huckleberry Finn*.

In the 1970's, books concerning Twain and his work give *Tom Sawyer* only minimal attention. A special instance is Serrano-Plaja's

*"Magic" Realism in Cervantes: Don Quixote as Seen Through Tom Sawyer and the Idiot* (University of California Press, 1970), which concentrates on Cervantes and adds little to our knowledge of Twain's work. Justin Kaplan's *Mark Twain and His World* (Simon and Schuster, 1974) barely mentions *Tom Sawyer*, although it is an excellent introductory biography otherwise. Meanwhile, interest in *Tom Sawyer* remained high if its steady sales in mass-market paperback form can be taken as indicative.

Occasional essays of interest about the book continue to appear. Elmo Howell's "In Defense of Tom Sawyer" (*Mark Twain Journal*, 1970) reduces claims as to why Twain wrote the novel to merely that "it was to relive his youth spent in a vanished world...." Treating in depth the relationship of Twain to his father, a relationship of obvious importance to development of the book's hero, is the essay "John and Sam Clemens: A Father's Influence" (*Mark Twain Journal*, 1970) by Keith Coplin. Published in *Studies in the Novel* (Fall, 1971), Judith Fetterly's "The Sanctioned Rebel" suggests that Twain used Tom Sawyer as a rebel to point up the hypocrisy that St. Petersburg's adult population endorsed. She sees this as a pattern in the novel, although in the final pages Tom himself succumbs to this society. "Mark Twain's Requiem for the Past" (*Mark Twain Journal*, 1972) is an essay by Stanley R. Harrison which treats the nostalgia theme. Elmo Howell writes again about *Tom Sawyer* in an essay titled "Tom Sawyer's Mock Funeral: A Note on Mark Twain's Religion" (*Mark Twain Journal*, 1972), a piece which points out that "Although the idea behind the mock funeral in *Tom Sawyer* is comic, in developing the scene Mark Twain gives it a serious dimension."

Observing that Twain's personal attitudes are somewhat transferred to the attitudes and the behavior of the novel's hero is "Tom Sawyer and Mark Twain: Fictional Women and Real in the *Play* of Conscience with the Imagination" (*Literature and Psychology*, 1973), an essay by Steven Karpowitz. The alternating scenes of play and reality are examined by Virginia Wexman in her essay, "The Role of Structure in *Tom Sawyer* and *Huckleberry Finn*" (*American Literary Realism*, 1973). Also, in 1973, Lyall Powers published "The Sweet Success of Twain's Tom" (*Dalhousie Review*), in which Powers concludes: "*The Adventures of Tom Sawyer*, from its disarming surface to its alarming depths, is as American as quick-frozen, ready-mixed, 'home-made' apple pie. And in the appeal of its telling authenticity it is a major reflection of ourselves." In "'I Never Thought We Might Want to Come Back': Strategies of Transcendence in *Tom Sawyer*" (*Modern Fiction Studies*, 1975), Tom H. Towers takes a serious look at the novel and finds it does not contain "the idyllic solution so often imputed to the book."

Published first in 1972 in a political science journal, "Tom Sawyer: Hero of Middle America" was made a chapter in Harry V. Jaffa's volume *The Condition of Freedom: Essays in Political Philosophy* (John Hopkins University Press, 1975). Jaffa says, "Tom Sawyer, master of the noble lie, is the master figure of American literature, the character in whom, more than in any other, Americans fancy themselves to be reflected and idealized." Brief reflections are made on "How Tom Sawyer Played Robin Hood 'By the Book'" (*English Language Notes*, 1976) in a short essay by Alan Gribben of that title. Alan Henry Rose, in his book *Demonic Vision: Racial Fantasy and Southern Fiction* (Archon Books, 1976) examines *Tom Sawyer* as Southern literature in his Chapter Four, "*Tom Sawyer*: The Making of a Safe World."

The centennial year of *Tom Sawyer's* first publication, 1976, produced several items. Having been in print 100 years, and read by so many millions during those years, the work deserved much more attention than the media provided. Although some will always see the work only as a juvenile item, many more scholars are sure to recognize its importance to Twain's career. An example is Dennis Welland's *Mark Twain in England* (Humanities Press, 1977), which presents among other things a number of new and useful facts regarding the English publication of *Tom Sawyer* in one of its chapters (a book made up in part from earlier items by Welland, including "A Note on Some Early Reviews of Tom Sawyer" published in 1967 by the *Journal of Americans Studies*.)

A significant step forward in investigative research was accomplished with the edition of *Tom Sawyer* published in 1979 as part of Volume 4 of *The Works of Mark Twain* (see end of Chapter 12 for other details). This is especially true of the useful Introduction prepared by John C. Gerber. Supplanting research by other scholars writing of this novel, particularly Blair and Hill, and adding a section titled Textual Apparatus to the edition, Gerber presents creditable evidence for Twain's having begun writing on *Tom Sawyer* during the winter of 1872–1873. However, by overlooking other evidence and using less original insight, Gerber conforms to the common theory that the author composed most of the last half of his novel during 1875. This is foremost of several points built on debatable premises. The supplemental materials included as a part of this Iowa/California version of the work are extensive and valuable to students of *Tom Sawyer* and Mark Twain. Faults with the work are that none of its material is indexed and parts are difficult to follow without copies of the original manuscripts, unavailable to the average student.

Future worthwhile criticism of *Tom Sawyer* will benefit from closer readings of the book's text, leading to a realization that its entertainment qualities deceptively cover its essential and important themes, that the book has a vital relationship to its historical background, and that this novel has a unique importance to the author's artistic development and achievements, most importantly as it is related to his more widely acclaimed novel, *Huckleberry Finn*.

# 15. "Tom Sawyer, a Drama"

Albert Bigelow Paine, in a caption in his Mark Twain biography, stated that *Tom Sawyer* was "begun as a play about 1872." Paine presented only the first page of a manuscript and nothing more to substantiate the claim. Paine may have lacked proof, but his theory has some logic.

There is no doubt, whatever, that Twain was attracted to the theater in his boyhood and throughout his life. There were times when the theater assumed greater importance than at other times, sometimes even dominating the author's activities. Although, for most of his career, it was a secondary concern compared to his writing for publication.

Beginning with minstrel shows in Hannibal and other traveling troupes, then attendance at the theater while living in New York, St. Louis, New Orleans, and San Francisco (writing drama reviews as a newspaper reporter at this last), he enjoyed theatrical performances and the company of theatrical people all of his developing years. As a lecturer, first in 1866, then off and on for most of his remaining years, Twain became a part of the theater as a performer himself. Thereafter, as an author and lecturer, wherever he traveled he maintained his relationship to the theater, cultivating the friendship of actors, playwrights and producers at every opportunity. He made one brief venture into public theater as an actor; at home he frequently accepted roles in plays concocted by his young daughters.

But, as an author, his strongest approach to the theater was his various attempts to create written material for dramatic productions. Led by his flair for humor and satire, his occasional attempts to write for the theater relied heavily on the use of burlesque techniques in nearly every instance. There is evidence he made his first effort to write a drama while still in San Francisco, believing he could improve upon some of the dismal attempts he witnessed there as a reviewer. Also, weeks before Elisha Bliss signed him to a contract to write *Innocents Abroad*, he had first begun to turn the experiences of his Holy Lands trip into a stage play. The initial use of Mark Twain's writing for a full-fledged stage presentation came with the production of a stage version of *Roughing It*. All evidence of that production, however, suggests it used little of the book's actual contents beyond appropriation of part of its theme and the work's title. Its prime aid to the author was in providing him with firmer ties to the theatrical world and certain of its people. Although other hands had written that play's script, it heightened his personal desire to write material for the stage.

A fortunate opportunity soon followed, his first and only notable triumph as a writer for the theater. Actually, it proved to be more of a financial success than an artistic triumph. This originated in 1874 as

Twain was in the midst of writing some of the major and important parts of what became *Tom Sawyer*. The occasion took place in early June of that year as he learned about a play based upon "Colonel Sellers," the chief character he had created for the novel *The Gilded Age*, coauthored with Charles D. Warner. When Twain learned that this play was being advertised and performed in San Francisco without permission, he immediately sent a letter to John T. Raymond, playing the lead role, and to Gilbert B. Densmore, the dramatist, telling them he planned legal action unless the performances ceased. At the same time Mark Twain began to develop a dramatization of his own for the Colonel Sellers character of that novel, who had been based on a cousin in part, his own father to a degree, and with touches of his own character present. After an extensive correspondence, an agreement was reached in which Densmore was paid for the work he had done, and Raymond, following consideration of several other actors, was hired to continue the role of Colonel Sellers in the version to be produced in New York under Twain's name as the author.

What part of the work, as presented in New York's Park Theatre, was Twain's doing, how much was the adaptation of the material by Densmore, or how much came from whatever interpretation Raymond added to the part, has never been clear. The matter is clouded by a number of claims, statements, and counterstatements. Twain made the claim, "[I] entirely rewrote the play three separate and distinct times," but some believe that much of the arrangement of the drama's plot remained from the version which Densmore had first put together. Whatever the case, there is evidence that the version which reached the New York stage was heavily dependent on the dialogue Twain had originally put into the speeches of Colonel Sellers for the novel. Twain's contributions, not to slight the stage directions added to the material, were the most valuable ingredient toward the play's success.

When the play opened in New York, on September 16, 1874, following "several days in succession" that Twain spent demonstrating to the performers how he "thought the speeches ought to be uttered" (according to a letter to his brother Orion), probably overseeing last minute revisions, it became an instant success with theater audiences. As one of the more successful plays of its time, it earned over $50,000 for the author in the beginning, then at least $20,000 more during the 14 years it was annually renewed and played in various cities. Titled at the beginning *The Gilded Age*, it soon became known by the title of *Colonel Sellers*, a tribute to the popular character it featured and around whom the action revolved.

*Colonel Sellers* produced income enough to relieve Mark Twain's greatly overburdened living expenses for a time, but he felt he needed another successful book. When in the summer of 1875 he suddenly decided that *Tom Sawyer* was "finished," the author began to scheme as to how he might dispose of his manuscript without its being a total financial loss. One thought was that his friend Howells might help by turning the material into a work for the stage. It seems somewhat odd that he would propose this to William D. Howells as the latter's experience at this time was as limited as, or more limited than, Twain's own. Such an action seems to indicate that Twain, despite the success implied by *Colonel Sellers*, was still unsure of his own abilities to develop a suitable plot from *Tom Sawyer*, or felt he could not abridge the material as the stage required. He may have considered that Howells was more competent in this area; but among the author's acquaintances were a number of experienced theatrical personalities who would have been more likely targets for the suggestion. But he trusted Howells, and feeling so frustrated with the manuscript for *Tom Sawyer* and the state he thought it was in, having put so much time into it without the results he had planned for, he made the request to Howells both as a respected friend and as the only outsider who had seen the work to that point. As Twain's time was being applied only to several minor writing projects in various stages at the time, it is strange he did not characteristically plunge into the work himself, as he had demonstrated a willingness to with *Colonel Sellers*, and at other times.

There is some evidence that he may have had such an urge, for when he wrote his request to Howells, he also noted that he could not forward the Tom Sawyer manuscript for a critical reading since "I telegraphed my theatrical agent to come here & carry the MS & copy it." (This action produced the copyist version used for the English edition of *Tom Sawyer*.) Also, at about this same time, he put together a synopsis of the story, an outline which closely follows the narrative of the work's manuscript and suggests something of the intended conclusion that was never to be written. This was forwarded to the Library of Congress Copyright Office for Dramatic Works where it was registered on July 21, 1875, securing all dramatic rights for the author. Whatever his real intentions, or whatever work toward turning the material of *Tom Sawyer* into a drama was accomplished at this time, all was dealt a severe blow when Howells turned down the offer: "it wouldn't be a favor to dramatize your work. In fact I don't see how anybody can do that but yourself." The tone of Howells' letter, as usual, was polite — but the refusal was plain.

Later, with *Tom Sawyer*'s publication promised, Twain put aside the thoughts of a stage presentation, at least until the following year when the book was in the various stages of printing. During the summer of 1876, as he worked in the hilltop studio outside of Elmira, New York, he again thought seriously about dramatizing the novel, hoping it would duplicate the success of *Colonel Sellers*. This time he turned toward his friend Moncure Conway in England for assistance. In their correspondence the subject appears several times, indications being that various English dramatists had been approached to secure their aid in turning the book's material into a workable stage presentation. All these apparently refused the plan. Actresses were also named and sought out, Twain believing for a period the role of Tom could be best performed by a young woman. While nothing definite came as a result of these efforts, Mark Twain, freshly smarting from his publication disputes with Elisha

Bliss, filled with disgust for the Canadians who had pirated the novel, and irked by the many mixups with his English publisher, told Conway in December, just as *Tom Sawyer* was being issued in America, "if I can make a living out of plays, I shall never write another book." Twain must have felt this a real possibility at that moment; during the recent months past he had accumulated many notes and had wrote some rough drafts for several acts of a play based on *Tom Sawyer*.

Regardless of the vague threat to give up writing books, the author spent the next seven years producing three of his more important ones. Meanwhile, he began breaking his ties to the American Publishing Company. This eventually led to Twain's founding his own publishing firm with Charles Webster at the head. Among other duties assigned to Webster was working as the author's agent. Though all plans for a play about Tom Sawyer were put aside, he continued to have definite theatrical ambitions, collaborating with Bret Harte on a play titled *Ah Sin* about San Francisco Chinese. It reached the New York stage, but was quickly closed due to lack of audience support, the critics being totally unimpressed. Even Twain's biographer, supportive on many issues, wrote that the play was "neither coherent nor convincing...."

Resuming his enthusiasm, Twain next authored a play titled *Cap'n Simon Wheeler, The Amateur Detective*. Designated "a light tragedy," he had it copyrighted, but it found no backers among those producers approached. Another aborted attempt at play writing near the end of this period occurred when Twain finally made arrangements with Howells to collaborate on a play, *Colonel Sellers as a Scientist*. Once more, initially enthused, the author had Charles Webster actively promoting the work among various producers and actors for weeks, but to no avail. Fortunately, during these discouraging years of theatrical ambitions, he was working, off and on as the inspiration struck him, to complete *The Adventures of Huckleberry Finn* which would in time win him endless literary honors.

No evidence of any activity toward the making of another dramatization from *Tom Sawyer* is noted until early in 1884. About this time Twain spent several busy weeks fashioning a couple of plays that he reported on in a letter to Howells. He indicated he had completed "one 4-act play" (based on *Tom Sawyer*), plus "2½ acts of another" (based on *The Prince and the Pauper*). Twain again applied for a copyright on this version of the *Tom Sawyer* material, using another detailed synopsis, this following the play's script and differing in a variety of ways from the novel. A copyright was granted on February 1 of that year. Immediately, he had Charles Webster again talking to producers, his aspirations for success in the theater remaining high, as indicated from a letter he sent Webster. "If the book business interferes with the dramatic business, drop the *former* — for it doesn't pay salt; & I want the latter rushed." A month later he wrote Webster that "Tom Sawyer is *finished*; & it is a *good* play — a *good* acting play.... I never meant that this Sellers business should stand for a moment in the way or take precedence of Tom Sawyer," putting aside the play he had worked on with Howells.

Serious for a time about his new version, *Tom Sawyer, A Play in 4 Acts*,\* Twain insisted that Webster actively search for someone willing to back it financially, also instructing him to look for actors for the main roles. This dramatization of *Tom Sawyer* contains obvious burlesque overtones in its script, considerably more than in the novel. For this reason Twain instructed Webster to look this time for adults who might assume the roles of the children. Webster's efforts were unsuccessful. Augustin Daly, producer of *Roughing It*, rejected Twain's proposal:

> I feel that *Tom Sawyer* would not make a success at my theatre. After a very close reading I must disagree with you on the point that grown up people may successfully represent the boys & girls of your piece. Tom might be played by a clever comedian as a boy — but the other parts would seem ridiculous in grown peoples hands.

The total rejection the play received from those approached regarding it gradually diminished the author's consuming interest in promoting it. During the next months, as he founded his own publishing firm, readying *Huckleberry Finn* for publication, the book business again took precedence over theatrical ambitions. Only occasionally did Twain still find time to put out an order directing Webster to pursue something that might result in either *Tom Sawyer* or the *Sellers* play's being produced.

It was also, sometime during 1884, that a play about Tom and Huck first reached an audience, but it was not Twain's version. A resident of Wichita, Kansas, Mrs. Sallie J. Toler, wrote to the author to request permission to dramatize and produce the story for a church benefit. *Tom Sawyer*'s author replied and granted the request. Mrs. Toler's script seems to have made use of as much of the essential story as possible, indicated by the cast of characters listed. Her son, who played the role of Huck Finn, recalled the event in a Kansas City *Journal-Post* interview published March 2, 1930. He clearly remembered the dead cat he had had to carry as Mrs. Toler strover for realism. The novel had by this point reached its first noticeable level of popularity among readers, and was bringing Twain an increasing number of requests from various persons who wanted permission to dramatize the story. Only in the case of Mrs. Toler did he grant such permission freely, or at all until later, knowing her use was for a limited, amateur, charitable function.

Exactly a year after being turned down by Augustin Daly on the play, Twain wrote Howells on February 27, 1885, "I sold the right to dramatize & play Tom Sawyer on a royalty & it is to be exploited presently in New York." Additional remarks indicate this was an entirely different play, or at least a total revamping of his own by another playwright, for he wrote, "I have not seen the MS; so I don't know anything about it." Some commentators have wrongly assumed on the basis of this remark that he had lost all interest in the material.

\**Printed in full in* Mark Twain's Hannibal, Huck & Tom, *edited by Walter Blair (Berkeley: University of California Press, 1969).*

A few months later, in May and June, 1885, Miles and Barton, the play's producers, tried out *Tom Sawyer* in Yonkers, New York, and Hartford, Connecticut, playing several one-night stands elsewhere, using Mollie Ravel, a young actress Twain had suggested for the role, as Tom. The *New York Mirror* reported the author was traveling with the play's production company. This would indicate Twain was having a hand in the ongoing efforts to improve the working of the play. A critic viewing the production wrote in the *Mirror* on June 6, "it reads better than it acts." Whatever the play's failings, the producers decided to cancel the play during mid-June. Only a portion designated "the picnic scene from Tom Sawyer" realized Twain's hopes when it was presented in New York City that month as part of a special benefit performance.

The disappointment from this venture was to stay with Twain for a long time. When W.R. Ward, a manager for the Kitty Rhoades Theatrical Company, from Auburn, New York, wrote the author requesting permission in September of 1887 to advertise a dramatic version he had put together of *Tom Sawyer* as a play created by Mark Twain, the author flatly refused the proposition. Seeming to be at last convinced that the novel's qualities did not lend themselves to the requirements of the stage, Twain mailed a curtly written reply to Ward warning him against any attempt to stage the play. In a longer, but unmailed version of his reply to Ward, Twain bitterly complained, "You are No. 1365 ... 1364 sweeter and better people including the author have tried to dramatize Tom Sawyer.... That is a book, dear sir, which cannot be dramatized. One might try to dramatize any other hymn." There appears an important change of attitude here, for up until this time, as shown by most evidence, Twain had thought only of doing the dramatic version of his story using a heavy burlesque approach, rather than trying a serious rendering of the material. It seems apparent that he had always felt more comfortable handling the material with a heavy stress on humor.

Ward, ignoring Twain's warning, included a version of *Tom Sawyer* in Kitty Rhoades' repertoire of several plays during 1888. The *New York Dramatic Mirror* (a successor to the *Mirror*), in its June 2, 1888, issue reported Ms. Rhoades to be performing the role of the novel's hero. She was a popular actress whose company played a number of one-week stands in small-to-medium size towns, performing a different play each day. She registered an impression on a *Dramatic Mirror* critic viewing her performance in Reading, Pennsylvania, in December of that year: "Miss Rhoades as Tom Sawyer was a favorite and was frequently called before the curtain." That knowledge of such use of the material could have escaped Twain's attention is difficult to believe, but nothing indicates he knew anything about these presentations; or, if he knew, that he did anything about them. Neither did he know about several more adaptations done by others.

As *Tom Sawyer*'s popularity continued to increase, reaching more readers year after year, the novel was several times used to furnish material for middle-class theater productions. According to *Dramatic*

*Compositions in the United States* (volume 1, published in 1918), a production titled *The Bad Boy* was produced using items from *Tom Sawyer*, *Fanchon*, and *Uncle Tom's Cabin*. This strange concoction, termed "a serio-comic drama in 4-acts," written by Ada Russell, was produced in 1887 by Phillip S. Greimer. During 1888 there are records of performances being presented in theaters from Pennsylvania to Louisiana. In view of the play's title, it must have relied heavily on items from *Tom Sawyer*.

Histories of the New York stage note that plays titled *Tom Sawyer* were presented at popular theaters with one-week stands in 1890, 1891, and 1892. The origin of these is not revealed, but they appear to have been light renderings of the material making much use of certain of its burlesque qualities. Records indicate the use of adult male comics playing the roles of the chief characters. Another production, bearing the very odd title *Shadows of the Past*, was listed as having been adapted from the *Tom Sawyer* book. It was performed in 1898. Twain probably had nothing to do with these various uses of his novel. It is also unlikely that any productions developed from his own efforts at dramatizing the material. It is also apparent that none of these productions paid him for their use of the material.

Twain's own interest in dramatizing *Tom Sawyer* was evidently suspended during this period, and was renewed only near the end of the century, to a degree, when Paul Kester and William D. Howells began a collaboration with the intention of writing a dramatic version of the novel. Howells had already worked with Kester, his cousin, on dramatizing *The Rise of Silas Lapham*, one of Howells' more popular novels. Their collaboration on the *Tom Sawyer* play, however, must have ended before much was accomplished. Evidence for this is shown when on May 29, 1900, Twain consented to a new agreement with Paul Kester and a brother, Vaughan Kester, a minor novelist, to furnish them sole rights to dramatize the book. The agreement set June 1, 1901, as the completion date for the projected drama. Charles Frohman, a producer with a high reputation in theatrical affairs, was reported as holding an option for production of a play about Tom Sawyer by the Kesters for 1901 and 1902. Nothing suggests, however, that the play ever reached a stage of production. Whether the fault rested in the Kesters' not being able to create a suitable script or with Frohman's not being able to produce financial backing, is not known. But, by the time the deadline had expired, Twain was interested in another author's version of the material. Not until 1914 was a play titled *The Adventures of Tom Sawyer*, by Paul Kester (not including the brother's name), furnished a copyright.

It could have been that one of the obstacles the Kester version of the novel ran into was an ambitious musical production that came into being under the title *Huckleberry Finn*. In spite of its title, this play was based largely on material taken from the *Tom Sawyer* novel. While this interpretation was announced as a collaboration between Twain and Lee Arthur, apparently the extent of collaboration by *Tom Sawyer's* author did not exceed the granting of permission to Arthur for use of the material. A possible development is that Twain became dissatisfied with the progress being made by the Kesters, at the same time being impressed by the terms of a new offer. If it was not his own decision, then it may have been set up on advice from Henry Rogers, the Standard Oil executive aiding in managing the author's business affairs to help him escape the debts that had all but bankrupted him a few years earlier. Twain may have acted on advice offered by Rogers' attorneys in making the arrangements, the change of title being principally a means to avoid legal problems with the Kesters and Frohman.

In addition to the change in title, there were also some curious shifts in certain relationships. Becky Thatcher became a sweetheart of Huck Finn, while Amy Lawrence (the "jilted" girlfriend of Tom, according to the novel) was returned as Tom's romantic interest. All of the action is located in St. Petersburg, including a visit to a haunted house, a temperance picnic, the robber's cave, the courthouse square, and an expanded scene of the boys playing circus, all derived from *Tom Sawyer*. It was apparently the first musical version of the book, the music and lyrics being the work of McPherson and Brynin according to existing sheet music. The production details were handled by the partnership of Marc Klaw and Abraham Erlanger, talented producers of the first rank. The production used an investment of $60,000 by the time the first performance took place in Hartford on November 11, 1902. The staging of this musical was praised for its spectacular scenery and musical effects, supported by a company of eighty performers, according to reviews published in the *New York Times*, the *Hartford Courant*, and the *New York Dramatic Review*.

After a week of performances in Hartford, the musical was sent to Philadelphia and then to Baltimore, staying a week in each, but with the closing in Baltimore a statement was issued notifying those interested that the production was to be "reconstructed and sent on the road some time in January." By early 1903, however, a decision was made to abandon the production. The large cast and expensive scenery were part of the financial burden that helped this version suffer an early end. No further performances of this musical have been recorded.

Meanwhile, burlesque versions of the story's material continued to appear on the New York stage as an attraction for the audiences of the popular theaters. One such version, witnessed by Rodman Gilder in 1902, so completely disturbed the then young critic that he wrote Twain to protest the treatment given the novel. In 1944, in an essay published in *Theatre Arts*, ambiguously titled "Mark Twain Detested the Theatre," Gilder revealed that his "uninvited textual report" was read by the aging author who then "returned the documents with thanks and said he would not bring legal action, because the dramatist's crime was against the public rather than against the author." Gilder, in closing his essay, admitted that Twain had never actually detested the theater as suggested by the title of his piece.

By 1903 Twain's personal involvement with any attempt to

dramatize *Tom Sawyer* appears to have ended. His interest in the theater would continue until his death in 1910, but never again nearing the intense level it had reached during the dozen or more years between 1874 and 1887. It was an interest which had had its beginnings with his early childhood, his role-playing as "Robin Hood," staging mock battles with lath swords, or seeking attention when marching in temperance parades costumed with a bright red sash. It was an interest which grew in his adulthood to become at times a central, consuming interest. His sometimes zealous efforts to dramatize *Tom Sawyer*, prominent among all his other efforts to create dramas for the theater, although they met with failure, are a significant part of his life as a writer, and an important part of the history of that novel.

With its present status as a classic of American literature, and no longer protected by copyright, *Tom Sawyer* regularly is used as a source for dramatic material, but seldom with any more success than that known by the book's author. An effective transformation of *Tom Sawyer* to a dramatic work remains to be discovered.

# 16. *Tom Sawyer* on Film

The great hope Mark Twain had that *Tom Sawyer* might be transformed into a successful stage presentation, either through his own or another's efforts, brought continual disappointment. Probably because of copyright considerations, it was not until twenty years after the author's death that various stage adaptations of the story began to be produced. Until then, the only dramatic rendering available was that which Paul Kester had done with permission. The Kester version, *The Adventures of Tom Sawyer* (Samuel French, 1914), had both its title shortened and was revised in other ways when given its only first-class production in New York, in December 1931 at the Alvin Theater as a special offering for children.

By then Twain had become a popular author in modern Russia, and a children's version of the work was performed there, also in 1931. This presentation of the *Tom Sawyer* material used young actresses for the parts of Tom and Huck much as Twain himself had recommended, and as Mollie Ravel and Kitty Rhoades had actually done in their early stage presentations in America. With the passing of the copyright of the novel in 1931, dozens of playwrights began to construct plays based on the story and its characters. These all varied in their makeup, length, and quality, and were designed, except for a few instances, mostly for juvenile audiences. A great number of them are one-acts, usually based on a single important scene from the book, these being intended for use as school dramatic presentations. Of the several four-act versions written, only a few have seen publication, two of the outstanding instances among these being *Tom Sawyer* by Sara Spencer (Anchorage Press, 1935) and *The Adventures of Tom Sawyer* by Charlotte B. Chorpenning (Coach House Press, 1956).

Of the musical versions, some appeared ambitious in being directed toward adult audiences as well as children. One of these was an operatic production presented in Kansas City in 1958 and in St. Louis in 1961. Another and unusual version, *Livin' the Life*, used materials selected from all of Twain's Hannibal and Mississippi writings, with most of the emphasis on *Tom Sawyer*. It was presented on Broadway in 1957. In an attempt to provide popular, adult appeal, it presented Aunt Polly having a romance, and it allowed Tom to exclaim, "Damn!"

In every one of these later attempts to adapt *Tom Sawyer* to the stage the chief problem has been similar to the one that prevented Twain himself from accomplishing it. In the back section of the Samuel French publication of Kester's version, an unnamed hand explains: "In attempting to dramatize a great book, filled with character and incident, one is apt to become overwhelmed with an embarrassment of riches."

It might seem that of all the possibilities for dramatizing the novel, the motion picture screen might be most promising. The scope of the camera, the wealth of talent and financial resources available to the industry, as well as the vast technical resources it has displayed, would appear to add up to the only real possibility for success. Yet, in spite of all these apparent advantages, few good books become successful films. It has been the misfortune of *The Adventures of Tom Sawyer* to have remained with this majority following four attempts on film.

The first took place in 1917. Tom was played by Jack Pickford, the young brother of famed actress Mary Pickford. While he had some modest success in his own career, he was already 21, much too old and tall to properly represent the young hero of the novel when he undertook the role. The scenario used for the picture was written by Julia Crawford Ives. The filming was under the direction of William D. Taylor. The producers, Oliver Morosco Photoplay Company and Jesse L. Lasky, made a decision to divide the story into two five-reel films. The first was called *Tom Sawyer* and released through Paramount in December 1917. It covered the events up to the return of the "dead" boys from their pirate adventures. The second part was called *Huck and Tom; or, The Further Adventures of Tom Sawyer*. This, released to theaters in March 1918, used the graveyard murder, the trial, and incidents at the cave.

Although publicity releases issued to the general press stated these pictures were filmed in Hannibal, Missouri (the statement also appears in several later references to the films), there is no evidence of any sort that a motion picture camera crew went to Twain's boyhood town. The filming, by all indications, was done on location in California. Some of the stage settings were probably based on photographs requested from the Hannibal Chamber of Commerce.

The ten reels of black and white film, considered as a whole, covered many of the principal scenes from the story, but their lack of sound allowed practically no use of any of Twain's original words, beyond the few flashed upon the screen at intervals. The black and white film did not serve the book's appealing descriptive passages. Both of these disadvantages, and others, worked to obscure the finer points of Twain's work, especially some of the better humor, when viewers watched a pantomime performance accompanied by piano or organ music, selected and played to conform with the events appearing on the screen.

The next version of *Tom Sawyer* came to the screen in 1930, in a production by Paramount Publix Corporation, directed by John Cromwell. The screen writers credited with the script were Sam Mintz, Grover Jones, and William Slaven. This filmed version, while still limited to black and white photography, had sound. Although there are numerous minor variations, in general the script held close to the original story. Tom's role was played by 15-year-old Jackie Coogan, then a growing youngster who still retained some of the precocious mannerisms that had brought him stardom some years earlier. While Coogan gave a personable performance, his size and age (although he did not match the disadvantages of Jack Pickford) were not the best for a true interpretation of the character. Opposite to him, Mitzi Green, supplied with plentiful curls and pantelettes, was cast in the role of Becky Thatcher. Junior Durkin assumed the role of Huckleberry Finn with some success. As might be expected, much of Twain's original language used in the novel was dispensed with in the final script, although the film did retain some of the book's spirit and surely inspired new readers to turn to the book itself.

The third version of *Tom Sawyer* to be filmed was released in 1938. This picture was produced by the talented David Selznick and made use of the host of filmmaking technicians employed in his studio. Nearly $1.25 million were invested in this production, a sizeable amount of money for films of that period. Most important, for the first time it could draw upon the use of both sound and color. According to information released by the studio's public relations people, who were seldom expected to refrain from ballyhoo, a selection was made from among "25,000" young possibilities for Tom across the entire country. The boy selected came neither from Hollywood nor Missouri and had no experience. He was Tom Kelly, a young Irish lad from the Bronx, New York, 12 years old with bright eyes and pert expressions constantly crossing his face. In being selected, he must have shown much of the natural joyousness of the book's hero. Critical opinions of his performance as Tom vary, however — some acclaiming it, others finding it too contrived, held in check, lacking the spontaneous qualities of the book's Tom.

The sets, all studio constructed, were beautifully detailed, but obviously much too pretty to be real. The filming was directed by Norman Taurog, making use of a script adapted from the book by John Weaver. It was well known, that in all pictures listed under the name of David O. Selznick, Selznick was invariably the maker of the chief decisions. This picture was painstakingly researched and photographed with exceeding skill, using most of the best technical aids then available. It received considerable advance publicity, including an exhibit at the Museum of Modern Art in New York City which attempted to touch upon nearly every detail of its production.

Audiences had to wait 35 years before another producer, supported this time with $3 million supplied by *Reader's Digest* and United Artists, again undertook the task. This fourth film, by Arthur P. Jacobs, was released in 1973. It was the first of the screen versions to be done as a musical, utilizing popular music and songs composed by the famed musical team of Dick and Bob Sherman. The brothers also were coauthors of the film's script. Don Taylor was named as the director.

The producer and the director made a decision to film the picture in Missouri. They selected the small village of Arrow Rock at the state's center to provide most of the principal settings. Arrow Rock was thoroughly remade by technicians into the likeness of an 1845 village and was named "Hannibal," although it was far from an accurate replica of Twain's hometown. The decision not to use the novel's "St.

Petersburg" as the stated setting was a strange change that invites some explanation. Many of the scenes presented in this version were basically derived from incidents found in the book but usually placed in a different sequence and with their original emphasis changed. Twain's well-aimed satirical punches at the popular institutions of his boyhood, the church and the school, were all but eliminated in the filming, perhaps to avoid chances of creating any controversy, although lesser bits of the author's satire and humor do appear in brief instances. The characterization of Tom, in spite of the noticeable changes made in the story lines, was as a whole much like that of the hero of the novel.

An experienced movie and television actor, 12-year-old Johnny Whitaker performed well in the role of Tom. His age, fresh personality, red curly hair and mischievous facial expression provided a clever choice — quite approximating young Sam Clemens, Tom's real life model. Jodie Foster played Becky. Known professionals filled major roles, except for Huckleberry Finn, but the rest of the large cast came from the population of Arrow Rock. As the musical element helped increase the entertainment qualities of the film, it reduced, except for some minor instances, the dramatic values. It was certainly not the ultimate use of the *Tom Sawyer* material, though the picture succeeded as popular entertainment — with some enlivening touches of burlesque techniques that would have won Mark Twain's approval.

Other versions have been filmed in foreign countries, two by Russian filmmakers, another in Rumania, and possibly still others elsewhere.

Concurrent with the fourth movie, a specially made television version was presented to American television audiences. While it was 90 minutes in length (including the time allotted to the commercials), it omitted some of the most important parts of the book from its script, touching only briefly a few such as the whitewashing of the fence. With these serious oversights it lacked almost all of the book's original vigor and satire. Also, the 1973 film version has been purchased by television and was shown at least twice on that medium.

In the spring of 1982 the Soviets produced a three-hour, three-part television version of *Tom Sawyer*, which *Time* magazine (April 26, 1982) said was "astonishingly faithful to the spirit and detail of the book." The time allotted this presentation promises complete use of Twain's story. Use of a nine-year-old actor for the part of Tom and of a ten-year-old for Huck approximates the ages of the characters as created by the book's author. Whether or not it retains the book's atmosphere, realistically duplicates the settings, and adheres to Twain's satire remains to be discovered.

Certainly, if any dramatic version of *Tom Sawyer* is to approximate the atmosphere and other abstract qualities of the original work, it would have to make faithful use of the material. It would have to take note of Tom's love for his aunt as well as his trickery, the satirical vision of the town cannot be missed, and the moments of real horror that Twain furnished for Tom and Huck need to be dealt with effectively. It would have to show an insight for the adult themes that run through the book. Although an audience of children would be expected to view it, the successful *Tom Sawyer* film would need to win the approval of adults.

It is of interest that two attempts by filmmakers using *Huckleberry Finn*, important as that novel is in a literary sense, have also been watered-down versions tailored for juvenile audiences.

# Part IV

## *Status as a Classic*

# 17. The Simple Story

Walter Blair, in an introduction to a 1962 edition of *The Adventures of Tom Sawyer* (Houghton Mifflin), asks: "What *does* it say? This is an important question to ask about any piece of fiction."

The simplest statement to be made about *Tom Sawyer* is that it is the story of a "bad" boy who succeeds over the hypocritical "goodness" of his village.

On the surface of the book, Mark Twain holds close to this simple outline. The events from which the story is constructed are described by the author in simple and nonliterary language for the most part. The sentences are not elaborate, the story proceeds in a straightforward manner, unfolding in chronological order with only one brief exception. The time scheme is held to the limits of a single summer. The action is limited to the immediate vicinity of the small village of St. Petersburg. It is an easy book to read, therefore one readily suited to young readers.

Such an opinion of this book has its good points but is also deceptive. The least attempt to outline the simple story of a "bad" boy succeeding over the hypocritical "goodness" of his village will soon reveal that this novel is considerably more complex. It is actually composed of five distinct groups of events through which the theme is developed: (1) Tom's pranks, at home, in the church, at school, and with his friends; (2) Tom's romance with the new neighbor girl, Becky Thatcher; (3) the adventures connected to the trip made to Jackson's Island by the young "pirates"; (4) Tom and Huck's witnessing of the murder of Doc Robinson, which is blamed on the lowest class citizen, Muff Potter the drunkard, whose innocence is revealed by Tom's testimony in court; and (5) the hunt for Injun Joe and the hidden treasure of the criminal band, which results in Tom and Huck's becoming "rich" and "accepted" in the community. In creating each of these parts of the story, Twain managed to retain a certain simplicity, each being told with a degree of isolation, disturbed only by some occasional overlapping.

This simple outline of the story's structure follows the basic intentions of the author but of course neglects, or overlooks, some of the book's finer details. Among the several complexities or added "layers" some serious critics find deserving of recognition, many might simply be the result of the author's wide experience, his extensive reading, his sharp mind and his command of language — the result of his talents rather than a manipulation of his material for so-called deeper meanings.

It is obvious, as well as important to any understanding of Twain's work, that his talent was best suited to the writing of sketches, most of his books being in a sense collections of sketches, sometimes with a closely unified theme and sometimes without. It is most likely that the writing of *Tom Sawyer* began with the authoring of individual sketches. The first several chapters of the novel show definite evidence of this. *Tom Sawyer* might well have been begun by the author without thoughts of writing a novel in the usual sense. Although sketch-like in their construction, these chapters are important to the novel as a whole and serve it well because they are all devoted to one character, Tom Sawyer, and to a unified theme, making acceptable the normal "bad" boy as opposed to the unnatural "model" boy of nineteenth-century Sunday school literature.

Chapters i through viii of the novel, all probably developed from earlier sketches, are chiefly concerned with the pranks of Tom Sawyer, a typical "bad" boy as opposed to a "good" boy, Sid, and a "model" boy, Willie Mufferson. The only other events the author worked into these chapters are the incidental introduction to the romance with Becky Thatcher, and the initial appearance of Huckleberry Finn, which provides the reason for the midnight visit to the graveyard where the murder of the doctor is witnessed in the next part of the book. In composing these opening chapters, Twain extensively and humorously illustrated the point he wished to make, that a typical, so called, "bad" boy can be normal, loved, and acceptable. Not only did he wish to make this a general point, but it was a point important to his own life.

The sketches had most likely originated as efforts to counter the "Peter Parley" and "Little Rollo" types of depictions of ideal children, which he and other serious writers considered offensive to truth. There is the possibility that they resulted also in part from his reaction to the attempt of another author, Thomas Bailey Aldrich, to counter these ideal images with a novel, *The Story of a Bad Boy*. That work appeared in 1869 and Twain apparently read it shortly thereafter, and certainly once he had met its author in 1871. Twain had a strong disapproval for Aldrich's bland style of prose and may have deliberately burlesqued the Aldrich novel in part. This speculation is sustained by the fact that several of the scenes in *Tom Sawyer* reflect on similar scenes in Aldrich's book.

Also a part of these first chapters, and reflected in them, is Twain's long acquaintance with the stories by Benjamin Shillaber concerning Ruth Partington and her nephew Ike. Twain had first read these Shillaber stories as a youth and his attention to them continued. However, while these first chapters do reflect strongly some of the substance of the writings of both Aldrich and Shillaber, they make use of special materials definitely from Twain's own boyhood. Adding to these Twain's command of humor and language, one finds it easy to praise his efforts far above those who may have inspired him.

In Chapters ix, x, and xi of *Tom Sawyer*, Twain suddenly turns his attention away from the issues of childhood play and pranks to the matters of real life, using one of the strongest examples available to literature, murder. This turn from fun to horror introduces into the novel the murder of Doc Robinson, the wrongful accusation of Muff Potter, left defenseless by his dependence on alcohol, and the revelation of Tom's deep concern with conscience. It also serves to establish the presence of Injun Joe, whose principal role is as the villain during the later treasure hunting events. In this three-chapter part, Twain presents the first illustration of the "bad" boy, Tom Sawyer's, capacity to become a hero. Adding strength to these chapters, Twain deals also with the unreliability of myths and oaths in real life, the fears and feelings of Tom and Huck illustrated in dialogue and descriptions that clearly tranmit the tensions they felt.

These chapters also form the introduction into Twain's treatment of the blood and thunder plot. But, with Chapter xii, the author resumes Tom's romantic interest in Becky. The romance in *Tom Sawyer* is not distorted by the heavy-handed burlesque treatment of the earlier sketch, "Boy's Manuscript." That predecessor of the novel focused almost exclusively on the ups and downs of the self-confessed romance between Billy Rogers and Amy, the object of his romantic confusions, leaving it with an one-dimensional aspect. While humor is frequently injected into the romantic incidents featuring Tom and Becky in their story, burlesque has given way to nostalgia. Chapter xii, however, is a mixture of themes, for in addition to the romance more of Tom's pranks are revealed, and the chapter provides the excuse for the adventures of the boy "pirates" on their raft voyage to Jackson Island.

These adventures on the island, covered in Chapters xiii through xvii, contain some of the best writing of the novel. Chapter xvii is especially famous for the return of the boys, believed to have drowned, to St. Petersburg to witness the start of their own funeral. Discovered, Tom and Joe Harper are greeted with relief, welcomed back into the fold of family and neighbors, "accepted" as alive again. But, while these two mischievious boys are welcomed back, Tom needs to remind his aunt, "Aunt Polly, it ain't fair. Somebody's got to be glad to see Huck." The hypocrisy of the village is revealed, shockingly, but continues as the boys become heroes through their play.

Chapter xviii opens with a brief flashback to the island adventures, to conclude them. Tom is a "hero" among his companions at school, although Becky ignores him momentarily for the "Saint Louis smarty that thinks he dresses so fine and is aristocracy!" With Chapter ixx, the author has Tom proving his love for his aunt, the butt of so many of his pranks. Then, in Chapter xx, Tom is provided the opportunity to prove his love for Becky, the chapter ending with Becky's words of approval, "Tom, how *could* you be so noble." Tom has taken the first step to overcome the "bad" boy image and to gain the first mark of acceptance with the donning of nobility.

The next two chapters, xxi and xxii, are mostly transitional passages and add practically nothing to the main themes of the book. But Chapter xxiii once more takes up the events connected to the graveyard murder as Muff Potter is brought to trial in the village courtroom for that deadly deed. Here, ignoring a part of the vow made with Huck on the night of the murder, Tom decides to testify and tell what he actually saw happen in the cemetery at midnight, moved to speak by his "troubled conscience." At this point Tom becomes a genuine hero as Muff Potter is acquitted and the actual murderer of the doctor, Injun Joe, makes a hasty exit. Tom is "a glittering hero once more" while "the village paper magnified him," and as the town "took Muff Potter to its bosom and fondled him as lavishly as it had abused him." These are strong words for a children's book.

With Injun Joe escaped, Chapters xxiv through xxvii once again take up his burlesque of the blood and thunder novel, dealing directly with the theme of the buried treasure and the hunt for the real criminal. These chapters take on a character quite different from the earlier chapters, and in them Tom and Huck seem to have grown in years, and slightly in maturity, but apparently only a few months have passed since the events of the book's opening pages.

In Chapter xxix, Twain separates Tom and Huck, Tom going on a picnic outing with Becky to the area of McDougal's cave, Huck still pursuing Injun Joe. The picnic and the entering of the cave by the frolicking children set the stage for the heightened aspects of Tom's romance with Becky while providing a place for the discovery by the book's hero of real "treasure" and the inglorious death of Injun Joe, a real "pirate." It also is a chapter in which Huck assumes for the first time an importance to the story nearly equal to that of the main hero. These matters are pursued further in Chapter xxx, as Huck after tracking Injun Joe to the home of the Widow Douglas goes to the Welshman for aid. Although an attack upon the Widow Douglas is averted, Injun Joe conveniently escapes again, while Huck is touted as a hero of the events. Huck desperately avoids having to reveal the identity of the "Spaniard" (Injun Joe in disguise) whom he had pursued, and why he had. For reasons not sufficiently explained, Huck becomes seriously ill as it is discovered that Tom and Becky are missing and probably lost in the cave, where the scene shifts next.

The Chapter xxxi adventures in the cave exhibit the author's finest creative skills as a writer of fiction. While many other parts of the story are constructed to a greater degree upon actual events from the author's own boyhood, his description of the events in the cave is almost wholly fiction. In addition to the highlight scenes of Tom's romance with Becky, this chapter allows the discovery that Injun Joe is hiding out in the depths of the cave. The chapter ends in suspense with Tom making a last desperate attempt to find a way out of the cave and defeat certain death.

Chapter xxxii finds Tom and Becky escaped from the cave—and Injun Joe's presence revealed, although he is even then sealed up in the darkness. The events pertaining to the freshly blooming romance between Tom and Becky, despite its heightened importance due to the fact that Tom has just saved her life, are abruptly concluded as a part of the novel. This sudden ending of any attention to this theme occurred because the author thought at one time that his work was only half completed having reached this point of the adventures and he had intentions to add at least another equal number of pages to the manuscript, though it is not clear how he intended to resolve the theme. Chapter xxxiii provides for the confirmation of the death of Injun Joe, allowing Tom and Huck to venture back into the cave through the small hole where Tom had escaped a few days earlier. Coupling perseverance and luck to the "clues" they have, the two boys uncover the hidden treasure of the vanquished robber band.

Chapters xxxiv and xxxv conclude the novel. Tom and Huck are revealed to be "rich" and accepted into the society of the village. But, at the end of the story, Tom is planning new adventures, telling Huck that he intends to form a band of "robbers." When Tom glorifies the intended adventures, Huck begs to join with Tom although it means he must endure the hypocrisy of Widow Douglas' world. It is now made clear to the reader that Tom has returned to his dreams and his obsessive desire for play once again. The facts of his heroism and wealth have become secondary, for essentially he is a part of the general hypocrisy in which he survives.

When Twain found that he was lacking the inspiration and desire needed to extend the tale, and had decided to agree with his wife and his friend William Dean Howells that what he had written was principally a story for boys as it stood, he added a brief "Conclusion." In this last he confesses, "the story could not go much further without becoming the history of a *man*." Still, it is a logical and satisfactory place to end the novel, with the boys, Tom and Huck, showing various signs of change or maturation to a degree. Interestingly to the moral tone of the book, there seems to be no change in the hypocritical village. In spite of Twain's problems with plotting, and several points where the story seems to wander from its course, interest is capably maintained throughout.

Twain's later statement that "Tom Sawyer is simply a hymn, put into prose form to give it a worldly air," provides the novel a simple description, but one that is far from sufficient. As far as it goes it is useful, for certainly there are those parts of the work that sing of a summer in childhood when things were simpler and play was the main objective. But, like the statements of the "Preface" and the "Conclusion," that description is a misdirection, for Twain must have had some realization that his work contained much more.

The nostalgic qualities of the novel are present, but they are successfully fused with the elements of adventure and humor in the total achievement. Each of these elements is present in a simple form on the surface, but together they form a more complex recollection of boyhood. Once readers have grasped that this is more than a simple story of boyhood, they can begin to examine the countless details delineated in the narrative and begin to study the motivation of the characters. In essence, the novel stands as a storehouse of those things that will always matter in boyhood.

During most of the writing Mark Twain believed it would be read chiefly by adults but after Howells' comments he devised the following thought for his "Preface":

Although my book is intended mainly for the entertainment of boys and girls, I hope it will not be shunned by men and women on that account, for part of my plan has been to try to pleasantly remind adults of what they once were themselves, and of how they felt and thought and talked, and what queer enterprises they sometimes engaged in.

# 18. Symbols and Substance

All writing is symbolism, more or less. The chief function of words is to act as symbols, some very precise, others shaded with layers of meanings. Strung together, words form more extensive symbolism, some intended by the author, some perhaps not. The question that needs to be asked is: "How much of the symbolism that is present in this work was intended?"

In the matter of *The Adventures of Tom Sawyer*, Mark Twain furnished only a few elusive clues. Further, only limited aid is gained by sorting out facts about his life and training. Because he regularly chose to present his ideas in the context of humor, on which he often placed a heavy emphasis, whatever Twain's intentions were in regard to what some critics consider certain interesting incidences of symbolism in *Tom Sawyer* will perhaps never be determined with any accuracy.

The symbolism found in this work beyond the simple story is vital to any understanding of why the novel is a classic. It is the symbolism that has made *Tom Sawyer* worth reading deliberately in search of more than an adventure tale. Although critics have not found nearly so much to write about *Tom Sawyer* as they have for *Huckleberry Finn*, since the latter contains many extended symbols beginning with the important one forming its foundation, the Mississippi River, nevertheless the symbolism in *Tom Sawyer* is worth more attention than it receives.

While Twain would appear not to have selected his symbols, rather allowing them to develop spontaneously, he must certainly have been aware of them from time to time. The subjects that he chose to write about and which make up most of the simple story are each vigorous symbols: the village, boyhood, romance, treasure, crime, and death. Each of these tolerate amplified interpretations. Whether Twain was aware of all that could be attached to these symbols, he managed to make good use of the simple meanings they hold for readers.

Surely the most important subjects for the book are the village and its people. To the boy hero the village is his world. To the author it may be a symbol of the world at large. The town upon which St. Petersburg was to a degree based supplied an excellent model for the purpose. When Twain was a boy, Hannibal was at the center of significant activities. There the American East formed a boundary with its West. Hannibal was on the boundary between civilization and the frontier where different values were often present and grinding together. It was essentially a Southern town, but it was a part of the North. As it was located on perhaps the most important highway of its time, the Mississippi River, the worlds of the river and of the land mingled there unsteadily, sometimes one dominating, then the other. Hannibal's medium size, essentially neither large nor small, allowed it to be a model of many towns.

In Hannibal young Clemens had ample opportunities to observe the hypocrisy, the joyful times, and the frightful times. He regularly saw both good and bad in people. He observed their greed and their concern for others, saw their foolhardiness and their intelligence. He viewed all these and put a bit of each into his story, sometimes in the proportion he found it, sometimes not. Because Twain used art to focus on actions in his story, he does not describe in detail the town where it is placed. One result is that he keeps his symbol pure. The real town, the more active and complex Hannibal that he knew, is only glimpsed from time to time in the novel's St. Petersburg.

While in *Tom Sawyer* Twain offered some strong criticism of the village, that criticism is tempered with humor and finally becomes secondary to it. If the novel is read quickly and without much reflection, the effect of the criticism is almost lost, certainly pushed into the background. The satire is often not so visible as that in *The Gilded Age*, but it is there, a part of the novel, and it deserves attention.

Not so secondary, however, is Twain's treatment of childhood, or more correctly, boyhood. (While the book is about as popular among girls as boys and while many of its feelings appeal to women as well as men, considering the spirit in which it was written, its era, and its author's own word for it, critical references still should be to "boyhood.") Among similar novels, *Tom Sawyer* outranks nearly all in this respect, its picture of boyhood incomplete but accurate. While most other boys of that literature seem wooden, Twain's seems live. Tom has a mixture of qualities, both good and bad, and many readers can see themselves in his character. While most all of the boy characters created by other writers in Twain's time have faded into a degree of oblivion, Tom retains a popularity and a freshness hardly diminished in over a hundred years of changes. The point at which *Tom Sawyer* is most the hymn, that Twain later claimed it was, is in its treatment of boyhood. It praises boyhood, lifts it from a minority status to one of importance, it glorifies its "summer" and creates a longing for its days of simplicity in matters of work and play.

It is small wonder that William Dean Howells, upon first seeing the manuscript for the novel, declared it was a book for boys. Although Twain had fully intended it to be a book for adults during most of its conception and creation, the viewpoint of the author is more narrowly that of a "boy" observer, than of an "adult" observer. The town and what happens in the story are almost exclusively described through the viewpoint of the boy and not the adult, but because of the symbolism that the book develops, the book is not a mere boy's adventure tale. The adult reader, seeing things through the boy, sees things with new values, things an adult might tend to overlook if not careful or honest. When the author stepped out of the boy character, as he did on a few occasions in the work, the change is obvious, disturbing, and surely the least rewarding parts of the book. Although it was to become an excellent example of a boy's adventure story, the fact remains that it was not originally written for this purpose. The novel contains a certain selection of words and language (even though Twain performed some later, but minor, revisions) intended to appeal to adult readers. Any reader, even the most demanding, can profit because Twain used the symbolism of boyhood quite differently than he might have if his intention had been to write only for boys.

The above discussion might also be applied to the symbol of romance in the work. Although the reasons are not completely obvious, Twain seems to be continuing his comments on the traditions of adult romances as he did more directly in the "Boy's Manuscript" that preceded *Tom Sawyer*. Yet, the antics of young Tom are so simple and natural that a reader can ignore any deeper meaning they might contain. Twain, adopting a typical Victorian morality as his guide, seldom made statements in regard to the sexual aspects of romance, and perhaps because of this approach, when young and "innocent" Becky is discovered sneaking a look at the teacher's book on human anatomy and the "stark naked" illustrations, the reader is all the greater shocked. Having made his point, Twain cleverly moves on to other matters.

The point in the novel where the romance is coupled to the adventures in the dark cave is exceptionally tender and beautiful. This is the high point of Tom and Becky's romance and for some readers it is also the high point of the book. Here Tom is driven more by his concern for Becky than by his own fear as he searches to discover a way out of the dark trap. In some motion picture versions of the novel the children are found by adults searching the cave, but the book's version in which Tom seeks and finds his own way out of the cave leads to an important bit of meaning — the need for self-reliance in romance. The need for Tom to become a self-reliant individual becomes apparent when it is learned that the majority of the adults had "given up the quest and gone back to their daily vocations." It is the strength of character he displays because his romance has helped him to mature that prevents his adventures from ending at the same point that Injun Joe's end. After his escape, Tom learns that as an afterthought the cave has been sealed with a "big door sheathed with boiler iron ... and triple locked." Injun Joe is thus trapped and dies a horrible death, but Tom and Becky have escaped a similar fate seemingly due to Tom's resourcefulness and his "childish" love for Becky. It is such ideas that make this treatment of romance succeed.

The simple romance of the children appeals to many readers. It can be credited perhaps to Twain's luck, for it was not his plan that the romance end as abruptly as it does in the novel. This came about because the work was completed short of its original goal, which would have required at least twice its present length. If this had not happened and Twain had followed the brief plot outline he had sketched out on the first page of his *Tom Sawyer* manuscript, allowing Tom to move from "Boyhood & youth" on through life to the fourth and last point of the outline, wherein the hero was to return home to meet again "The Adored Unknown a .... faded old maid & full of rasping puritanical vinegar piety," the symbolism of the book's romance would have developed a vastly different complexion.

What Twain does have to say about romance is not as clear as what he has to say about the other symbols touched upon in the work, but that is essentially true of his entire body of work. That he tends to make fun out of Tom's romance in the early stages might indicate that he held a low opinion of the shenanigans of men and women performed in the name of romance — perhaps even his own performance. At the same time he also seems to reveal a basic longing for the inspiration that romance can bring into life, and his treatment of the symbol in *Tom Sawyer* seems to move from the former opinion to the latter in the book. The value of his own childhood romance with Laura Hawkins may never be properly assessed, but it apparently served as a model for some of the early aspects of Tom's antics, and the fact that he felt required to make use of it late in life at the age of nearly forty, when *Tom Sawyer* was composed, suggests that it may have had a value for him greater than he was willing to express openly, and preferred to approach it through fiction rather than fact.

Very close to romance is money as a frequently used source for plots and symbols. Like many other authors, Twain makes use of money (in one or another form) in many of his stories. In *Tom Sawyer* he gave emphasis to a variety term, "treasure." A large percentage of blood and thunder stories revolve around treasure, and since one of Twain's purposes in writing *Tom Sawyer* was to create a satire on novels of that category, it was natural to give it a prominent place in the work. The desire for acquisition and effects of wealth are treated in the novel, but only as one theme among several. The author introduces the subject early in the novel at the low end of the scale with reference to items that have almost no monetary value, creating the scenes about the "stealing" of sugar, the awarding of an apple, the "hooking" of a doughnut, and Tom's first accumulation of "treasure" provided by the whitewashing enterprise. Real money becomes the subject when the murder of the doctor occurs at the gravesite as Injun Joe demands more than five dollars in pay for their grave robbing undertaking.

The importance of accumulating wealth becomes more involved symbolically as the story turns toward playing pirates. With Chapter xxv, the symbol begins to become a major one. Twain states, "There comes a time in every rightly constructed boy's life when he has a raging desire to go somewhere and dig for hidden treasure." While at first it remains play for Tom and Huck, the quest suddenly develops into a search for actual treasure, following the revelation to the boys of the loot Injun Joe and his cohorts have accumulated. This introduces the events around the tracking of Injun Joe, the incidents of the adventure in the cave, and finally the discovery of the treasure's location after Injun Joe has met his fate. Thus Tom and Huck become the richest members of the village in terms of "actual cash." Each of the boys has an income of about $360 a year after their moneys are invested at "six per cent." Neither youth, however, is satisfied with their real wealth — nor Tom

with his hero status nor Huck with his opportunity to become a proper
member of society. Twain ends the story with Tom promoting a plan for
the boys to become robbers; Tom uses the term "high-toned" robbers,
represented by "nobility — dukes and such." As the book ends the author
is already into the plot of *Huckleberry Finn*.

Born and raised in near poverty, the acquisition of wealth became a
driving force in much of what Twain pursued in the years of his life.
Although he criticized various attitudes and actions of the wealthy, he
readily joined their society when the opportunity arose. The earning of
money in large sums was a prime purpose in the origin of many of his
books, *Tom Sawyer* being no exception. The way Tom collected his
wealth was similar to the way Twain operated, aided by persistence and
luck.

Certain of the business methods that Twain adopted to bolster his
income were sometimes dubious but never criminal. He was a foe of
crime according to the standards of his day, and spoke out strongly in his
writings and satires, especially *The Gilded Age*, against illegal pursuits
of wealth. Although the attack is less direct, it is also a part of *Tom
Sawyer*. Crime is a more integral part of that novel than most commentators have admitted. The petty *crime* of a bad boy is immediately con-
trasted to the most serious crime of all, murder. Another phase of crime
is the court trial, a subject that finds its way into many of Twain's books,
and it is important to *Tom Sawyer* as a turning point in the plot as well
as a symbol. Various aspects are commented on: the accusing of the
wrong person, the reluctance to reveal the true criminal, the petition of
a misguided committee to seek a pardon, a pardon made unnecessary by
Injun Joe's grisly, ironic death — an end some could attribute to
providence, while others might see it the result of human error.

In addition to being a murderer, Injun Joe is also a habitual robber,
a member of a gang of criminals. He is narrowly prevented from com-
mitting another crime, an apparent attempt to harm the Widow
Douglas, an attempt that has all the appearances of a rape (although
Twain avoids use of the term). All of this crime symbolizes the surface
crime familiar to the blood and thunder novel that Twain was intent
upon satirizing. Yet surely he wanted his symbols to suggest deeper
layers of the subject — the readiness of the people to condemn the *visible*
crime, to elect themselves vigilantes, and to attach a certain roman-
ticism to criminals, in contrast to the more subtle crimes of society,
which is only hinted at remotely in *Tom Sawyer*, but which had been
elaborately illustrated in *The Gilded Age*. Perhaps the author had
stronger intentions, and if he had been able to carry out his original
plans for writing a longer novel he might have treated this type of crime
in a more revealing and critical fashion as he followed the careers of his
characters. That he did not do so, leaving his use of the symbol less forceful than it was in the earlier novel, does not make the symbolizing of it
any less important to an understanding of *Tom Sawyer*.

Twain was no stranger to crime in its many forms. He had seen
various crimes as a boy in the streets of Hannibal. His father had been a

county judge and a justice of the peace. Twain must often have observed some of the local trials held by Judge Clemens in his small Hannibal courtroom. The sentiments which he expresses in *Tom Sawyer* had their beginning in this experience. Later experiences reinforced the earlier as he began to observe other and similar forms of crime along the river, in the West, and during his ventures into Washington. As a newspaper reporter he again had many opportunities to be an observer of the actions of the courts. Some of his treatment of crime may be objective, some subjective, but it is always a dramatic treatment and an important part of his tale.

Since violence often accompanies crime, we find a good share of it in *Tom Sawyer*, again more than some readers have been willing to see. The violence takes several forms, but the most important is death. Twain experienced intimately many deaths, including those of two brothers, a sister, his father, and shortly before he commenced to write the sketches that form the opening of *Tom Sawyer*, an infant son. Violence resulting in death was never too far away in early Hannibal. In turn, death by murder, drowning, hanging, disease, accident (trapped in a cave), knives and guns is all either prominent or hinted at in St. Petersburg of the novel. As a symbol, death is nearly always present in *Tom Sawyer*, and the overcoming of it becomes a basic part of the story, one of the items that makes the book attractive as a classic.

The murder in the cemetery, basic to the plot and the satire of the blood and thunder adventure story, has been suggested, since it is a doctor that is murdered, as reflecting on a long-standing grudge Twain was said to bear for the doctor who performed an autopsy on his father, witnessed accidentally by the author in his boyhood. While this is psychologically plausible, and cannot be ruled out, the incident might also be more symbolic of desires to expose for criticism those doctors, often charlatans in the small towns of Twain's boyhood who profited from deceiving those who trusted them, and occasionally from robbing a grave. Twain's portrayal of a boy's attitudes toward death are not always perfectly clear, but neither is a boy's clearer, and his approach to the subject is an ample challenge to the distorted picture normally found in the "good boy" literature and lesser adventure tales.

The symbols of "midnight" and "thunderstorms" can be aligned with death as a symbol, but although these occur with some regularity in *Tom Sawyer*, like a background chorus, they are never exploited to their possible depths. They remain in the background as they were in the background of Twain's own youth.

However, developed with a touch of satire and some of the author's best humor, the treatment of the "funeral" needs special recognition. The scene created in Chapter xviii, though only a few pages in length, is one of the most memorable in all of Twain's work, and particularly one of the high points for the readers of *Tom Sawyer*. Drownings were a frequent part of life in a river town and funerals at which there was no corpse must have been a regular matter. Twain recreates the apparent solemnity of a scene such as he could have witnessed more than once.

There is even a chance he may have known of such an event in which the victim, or victims, walked into the church in the midst of a funeral service. Whether or not based on a true event, Twain's use of the return from death adventure provides a vivid resurrection scene. The irony expressed by the return of the living bodies is calculated.

As clear as this and his other symbols seem, we cannot always be sure of what he wished to emphasize when using them. No commentator has ever been able to exhaust all the possible meanings. As simple as the structure of the story is, there is little doubt that Twain used his humor only as a trimming, that it was not the prime substance of his writings. More than once he hinted they were written basically to expound various parts of his moral beliefs.

Several instances of literary symbolism can readily be traced to Twain's absorption of the classical writings he read from time to time, especially during the years he worked on the river. What we hear occasionally in *Tom Sawyer* are the echoes of these themes in the author's mind.

Intentional symbolism, or not, their presence in *Tom Sawyer* has established a basis for the attention that several scholars have given the work. Olin Harris Moore's notice of the influence of Cervantes' *Don Quixote* on Twain brought some of the first serious attention given the work. Moore's points are well argued, as are those of Walter Blair in "On the Structure of Tom Sawyer." Kenneth S. Lynn, notes even more extensive use of symbolism in the novel; the ideas of Albert E. Stone, Jr., are general but also enlightening; while Frank Baldanza's interpretation in terms of "guilt cycles" seems to read more into the purposes of the author than was likely to be there. Robert Regan noticed a trace of the "unpromising hero" theme in the book, and James M. Cox treated the themes of the work's dramatic complexion in another analysis. Regan and Cox concentrate on the technical aspects of the writing, defining things that are evident to critics but hardly a result of the author's intentional choice. These sorts of theories are likely to be ignored by the general reader seeking entertainment from the work. But each critic adds something to the accumulating knowledge of the work and to its interpretation and thus each deserves a fair hearing and should be read by anyone wishing to form their own interpretation of *Tom Sawyer*.

Opinions of Mark Twain may change, but it is unlikely that those surrounding *Tom Sawyer* will vary greatly from those of the present. His success as a humorist is definite and well deserved. So long as the novel continues to be read, Twain can be expected to maintain his reputation as a humorist, for its humor is what appeals most to most of its readers.

# 19. The Making of a Classic

When a book is established as a classic, the reasons may be various, and while some may be obvious, others remain more subtle, and many are quite inexplicable. Sometimes it happens in a rather short period of time, as was the case with *Tom Sawyer*; but more often it takes longer. Those works adjudged to be classics usually retain their high status for a long time, but inevitably some lose their original lustre and are neglected.

*Tom Sawyer* someday have be among these last, but not in the immediate future. In the 1980's it is still a popular book.

Mark Twain's reputation does not rest on any perfection he exhibited as an author of extended narratives. Even his most universally regarded novel, sometimes placed first in the ranks of American literature, has faults in its construction that continue to be debated. While *Huckleberry Finn* is superior to *Tom Sawyer* in its depth and fuller explication of its character, the use of a greater number of scenes and more complex incidents, *Tom Sawyer* displays a firmer structure as a novel (even with its several faults). But Twain's outstanding ability to create short segments was his greatest attribute, and it is for those special parts of *Huckleberry Finn* that are so finely wrought that he deserves the praise given that work.

The flaws of *Tom Sawyer* create no great problems but an honest critic cannot overlook them. They are not so significant that they interfere with the values of the story, but neither are they so invisible that the careful reader will not be aware of several of them. Every classic contains a few flaws, their reputation resting on things other than perfection. Flaws aside, classics are notable for their treatment of their subject matter, the uniqueness of their narrative, the strange and exciting details they offer the reader, the insight they present through their characters and situations, their mastery of language, and more. *Tom Sawyer* is not one of the more esoteric examples of a classic; nor is it, properly understood, one of the simpler.

First there is the plot, or the lack of one. *Tom Sawyer* has only a simple plot, as noted earlier. The "bad" boy who succeeds over the hypocritical "goodness" of his village is the all encompassing cause for the selection of events in the story. This is developed through the presentation of a number of adventures in which the hero and his friends, particularly Huck Finn, manage to survive a series of crises, some very minor, others major. Though the various adventures are related, the relationship is slight and each is permitted an individual importance that stands out from the central crisis of the book.

The first individual crisis is highlighted by the murder the boys witness in the cemetery at midnight. From this they retreat with troubled attitudes. The next is the series of adventures surrounding their visit to the island as they leave their village "intent" on becoming pirates. This is resolved simply, after some moments of suspense, when the boys return in a melodramatic but humorous scene. The third crisis is presented in a minor key, but is important. It results from Tom's romantic feelings for Becky and her brush with near disaster when she tears a page in the teacher's anatomy book. This crisis is tactfully resolved when Tom takes her punishment.

Yet another crisis then ensues, related to the graveyard murder, as Tom struggles with his conscience and finally testifies to save the wrongly accused killer and reveal the actual one, Injun Joe. A closely related crisis follows next, one of heightened suspense, marking an increased intensity in the novel. This crisis builds through a series of events, Tom and Huck beginning with a "game" of hunting pirate treasure. The game becomes serious after they enter the "haunted" house where they discover Injun Joe and are in turn almost discovered by him, in a tense scene. Revealed also in this section is the real treasure that leads the story to its eventual climax. The next two crises branch from a single point as Tom and Huck search for the new hiding place of the robber's loot. The novel continues in its heightened mood of suspense, first as Tom nearly steps on Injun Joe in a dark room at a shabby tavern, then as the boys move into separate adventures. Huck, for the first time alone in the spotlight, becomes a hero as he dogs the criminal and a companion to prevent an attack on the Widow Douglas.

Meanwhile, Tom and Becky wander deep into the cave at the picnic grounds and get lost. Their crisis grows as their last candle burns out and they know they are in serious trouble. Here the story reaches its highest moment of suspense in one of the most well-written episodes in the book, perhaps in all of Twain's fiction. But, just as a tragic end seems a reality for the young pair, Tom discovers that Injun Joe shares the depths of the cave with them. Frightened and desperate, he searches for a way out of the dark passages. The resolution of this outstanding crisis takes place in the next chapter when it is discovered that Tom and Becky have arrived safely back into the village following Tom's discovery of a small opening far from the main entrance to the cave. It is the second and most important time in the story that Tom, after being believed "dead," has returned to "life."

The climax of the story begins as Tom and Huck return to the cave by means of the small opening Tom had discovered in escaping. Injun Joe, having been found dead at the sealed entrance to the cave, no longer stands in their way as they return to the cave to uncover the treasure cache. After having violated the petty, routine hypocrisy of the village several times, Tom's adventures come to a halt, not on a heightened level in which everyone "lived happily forever after" but on the level of ordinary reality. Although Tom and Huck are greatly enriched as the veterans of several exciting adventures and now the wealthiest pair in the village, their magic summer closes as they turn their backs on reality and revert to matters of play again. The circle is closed, the novel completed. Those who defy the hypocrisy of the village are rewarded — but they do not escape nor make any significant change in the village.

Twain's handling of the plot improves as the novel advances, but he seems to have full control only through the last couple of chapters. The author leaves an array of loose ends, in part, the result of the opening portion of the novel. In the first eight chapters, there is very little writing that helps to establish or advance the plot of the novel. These chapters retain the nature of the sketches out of which they grew. As Twain wrote them, and later applied them to his novel as the starting point for an attempt at creating a satire of the blood and thunder novel, he had no clearly established plot line. Later, after the plot of the novel was established, he added only a minimal amount of connecting matter, leaving the original character of the material only slightly altered as the final revisions were made in the manuscript. Twain's intentions for this material varied from time to time and signs of this remain in the construction of these chapters.

Originally, he created only satire sketches on boyhood, likely developed from monologues created for his lecture engagements. Put together, these became an attempt to counter the "good boy" tales of Sunday school literature with a glorification of a "bad" boy who is a normal boy, and a challenge to Aldrich's own handling of *The Bad Boy*. Next, they were considered as a group of chapters of a proposed picaresque novel when the author had visions of developing such a longer work. They were set aside after Twain undertook the coauthoring of *The Gilded Age* with Warner. They remained undisturbed until Twain set out to write a satire on the blood and thunder literature in 1874. Finally, when that project did not develop into the long novel that the author had anticipated, they became the opening section of the shorter novel as published. By January of 1876, when Twain did his final revision of the manuscript, only minor revisions of them were necessary. While those first eight chapters of the book are low in plot content, they serve a useful purpose in establishing the character of Tom and creating a concerned interest in him.

Granting that Twain never was among the more able and careful writers of long narratives, many of the gaps and faults in the novel can be laid upon the length of time involved between the penning of the sketches and their final adaptation into the novel. Most always writing with the help of inspiration, and only occasionally putting himself on a daily schedule (his longer stretches of sustained work often disrupted by other matters), Twain often would lay aside manuscripts, as he explained later, for his "tank to fill up again." This inconsistent schedule took its toll, and a large part of the faults in the plotting and narrative line of *Tom Sawyer* resulted from this practice, as well as some of the more insignificant if troublesome mistakes.

The progress of the narrative, from the opening pages to its conclusion, is limited to one summer. Some critics have pointed out, after carefully timing the events, that the summer is abnormally long — which it is, though this is helpful to the development of the story. The most troublesome result is that Tom seems to grow from a child of seven or eight into a boy of 12 to 14 in the space of those magic summer months. This noticeable maturing of the character is cited by some critics, searching for the overall plan the author followed, and they contend Twain used it to hold Tom's adventures together. They theorize an attempt by the author to suggest the growth of his hero from boyhood to manhood. While such a maturing is evident in much of the novel, it is hard to believe that Twain was fully aware of it. Even if intended, it is difficult to develop from a clowning imp who loves childish games (including riding about the village streets on a wooden horse, an incident removed entirely from one manuscript but present in traces in the other) a courageous boy who saves himself and his companion from a terrifying fate, and at the same time pursues a hardened thief and murderer, ending with the successful discovery of a sizable treasure.

Many critics are troubled as they try to resolve the matter of the hero's age, but it never seems to trouble the average reader who is also not commonly disturbed by the lack of other information regarding Tom Sawyer. Tom, whom so many of these readers immediately recognize in the work of many illustrators, beginning with True Williams on through the realistic depictions of Norman Rockwell, is nowhere fully described physically by Twain in the book. His voice is loud and clear and his actions are amply reported, but hints as to his physical appearance are few and far between. The reader is supplied only such rare items as Tom's tendency toward curly hair, that he has the teeth of the infant which are capable of being removed by the "string-on-the-door" method, that he is not dressed in the finery of the "model boy" although his clothing is superior to Huck Finn's, that he sports on Sundays a "speckled straw hat" and tallow coated shoes which he will wear only over protests. Otherwise, the reader must imagine him healthy and suntanned as he plays and swims.

But, there are no indications that Tom is either short or tall, fat or thin, has blue eyes or brown, has blond hair or red (like his creator as a youth). He is just a typical boy of a typical village, old enough to go to school or play hooky, being raised in a Christian home (although the word Christian is never mentioned in the book). He has an aunt, a half-brother, and a cousin; none of them is ever described in detail either. His friend Huck Finn, the forbidden companion of village boys because Huck never goes to school or to church, receives only a brief description upon entering the story. Twain furnishes such a fascinating look into Tom's mind that the physical appearance becomes secondary.

The reader is not told how Tom became an orphan. There is no information given to confirm that he and Sidney shared the same mother or the same father. Beyond the point that Aunt Polly recognizes him as her "own dead sister's boy," no other information as to his parents is supplied, nor do either he or his half-brother Sid display any longing for their departed parents. Readers learn that Mary is a cousin of the two boys in Aunt Polly's house, but there is nothing to indicate whether she is Aunt Polly's child. Twain, apparently beginning with the intent of preparing monologues, simply never saw it necessary to add the additional details to the characterizations.

While he does not provide the physical details that might result in a clearer picture of his characters, Twain does provide certain items not vital to the outcome of the story that supply an air of reality and allow for a recognition of the passage of time. These are such events as those witnessed in the classroom, those which occur during Sunday school and the church service, those that take place on Examination Day, those related to the temperance pledging, and other more minor items that provide a background for the unfolding of Tom's adventures. The book would be certainly poorer without them, however slender their relationships are to the main story or plot.

A number of critics, and perhaps some readers, become disturbed by obvious errors which developed during the composition of *Tom Sawyer* and never were corrected in manuscript revisions or during the proofreading. A particular and unfortunate mixup surrounds the characters of Lawyer Thatcher and Judge Thatcher. Other characters appear, are used for the events at hand, then forgotten, such as the little slave boy Jim and Ben Rogers, the first of Tom's friends the reader is introduced to. After many references to the "Welshman" he becomes known as "Mr. Jones" thereafter. There are also errors that remain because they were copied by the typesetters without question and overlooked during the proofreading (which the author seldom tackled with anything resembling enthusiasm). In the original edition, for example, St. Petersburg is found spelled both with and without an "h" at the end, as it was in the handwritten manuscript.

Other problems originate from the manuscripts, the first being all in Twain's hand, the second being in the hand of a copyist for the most part. A limited number of errors can be laid to these two manuscripts, but these small errors disturb only the most sensitive reader. Most of the 100 or more differences — between the English first edition, set from the copy manuscript, and the American first edition set from the original manuscript — are minute. Those that are more readily noticeable, such as the "additional chapter" found in the English version, do not affect the story to any extent. Of all the errors which can be laid to the printers' work, most are also insignificant and a closer coordination with final revised manuscript would have helped to eliminate the majority of them. Although these errors, all taken together, are troublesome to the specialist who reads the novel closely, word by word, it is probable that few average readers have suspected their presence.

Not only has this novel become a permanent part of American life, its chief hero has also, independently. The experiences of Tom Sawyer are those of a boy growing up on the frontier of Missouri about the year 1844. But there is something greater about him that is very modern. Perhaps it is this that has kept the book and its hero so popular and continues to make them important today. Tom Sawyer is not unlike those heroes of the present — a lover of independence, one imbued with romantic ideas, a supplier of new ideas, a leader, an individual who has bucked the system and found success.

# Appendix I

## The Manuscripts

In a letter to William Dean Howells on July 5, 1875, Mark Twain described his *Tom Sawyer* manuscript, "It is about 900 pages of MS., & may be 1000 when I shall have finished 'working up' vague places...."

Howells offered to read the manuscript, but its author "weakened" and reported to Howells, "I telegraphed my theatrical agent to come here & carry off the MS & copy it."

No more is heard about the original or the copy that resulted until late in October 1875 when at last the copy was offered to Howells to read. "Say, boss, do you want this to lighten up your old freight train with?" a skeptical Twain flippantly asked. Then, several days later, he informed Elisha Bliss to allow True Williams, illustrator of the American edition, whatever part of the original manuscript the artist wanted, indicating that the American Publishing Company had taken possession.

Howells finished reading the copy manuscript about the middle of November, writing to the author, "I have made some corrections and suggestions in faltering pencil which you'll have to look for." When Twain received the manuscript from Howells late in November, troubled by his health and the persisting opinion of Howells that it was a "boy's story," the package was laid aside unopened until mid-January, 1876.

At that point Twain hurriedly revised the copy manuscript, having made arrangement with Moncure D. Conway to oversee the publication of an English edition of the novel. About this same time the author undertook the task of trying to make the original manuscript agree with the changes. When Conway sailed to England on March 9 he took the copy manuscript and eventually made arrangement with Chatto & Windus for publication there.

Beyond the point of publication of the English edition in June of 1876 and the American in December of that year, the fate of the two manuscripts can be only outlined until they arrived at their present locations.

### The Copy Manuscript

The 654 page copy manuscript is mainly in the hand of two unknown copyists. It also retains the penciled notes by Howells. In the Twain's hand are the "Preface" and the "Conclusion" along with much evidence of revisions.

151

It appears that following publication by Chatto & Windus the copy manuscript was returned to Moncure Conway. It was to remain in his possession until his death in 1907 when it was removed from his estate to Charles Scribner's Sons in New York City. It was to remain there for a number of years until transferred to Frank Glenn, a rare book dealer in Kansas City, Missouri.

Dates are unknown, but thereafter it followed a circuitous course. First it went from Glenn to Fred Allsop and from Allsop to the Parke Bernet Galleries. Next it went to Leo Weitz whence it was returned to Frank Glenn, who loaned it to the University of California, which was considering its purchase. Failing there, Glenn finally sold it to the State of Missouri in 1950 for $7,500 (a price which included a Millet portrait).

At times termed "the English manuscript," sometimes "the Missouri manuscript," the copy manuscript was first exhibited in the Capitol building in Jackson, Missouri. With the 1961 dedication of the Mark Twain Memorial Shrine in Florida, Missouri (the author's birthplace), it was placed in a display cabinet there.

The pages of the copy manuscript are mounted on larger sheets and bound into a leather covered book that also contains some of the correspondence of Conway with the author.

## The Original Manuscript

The American Publishing Company did not return the original manuscript to Mark Twain following publication. Why, and how long it remained at the company, is not known.

Although Elisha Bliss died in 1880, his sons, half-brothers Frank and Walter Bliss, held positions with the firm thereafter. There is no record of the author's having requested from any of them the return of his manuscript. When Walter Bliss died in 1917, it was reported to be a part of his estate. Between then and October 1926, its whereabouts are not clear, but at that time it was purchased at an "open auction" by a wealthy New York businessman. Nicholas F. Brady, chairman of the board of the New York Edison Company, held the manuscript until his death in 1930. His widow then placed it with the A.S.W. Rosenback firm, but no sale was concluded. In 1934 Mrs. Brady decided to present the original manuscript to Georgetown University in Washington, D.C.

It remains a part of the Special Collections of that University's library, the 876 pages preserved in transparent protectors and bound in red morocco.

In the latter part of 1982 a two-volume photographic reproduction of this manuscript was published by the Georgetown University Library and University Publications of America.

# Appendix II

## Chapter Numbering in Three Editions

| English first edition | Canadian first edition | American first edition |
|---|---|---|
| I | I | I |
| II | II | II |
| III | III | III |
| IV | IV | IV |
| V | V | V |
| VI | VI | VI |
| VII | VII | VII |
| VIII | VIII | VIII |
| IX | IX | IX |
| X | X | X |
| Xᵃ | XIᵇ | XI |
| XII | XII | XII |
| XIIᶜ | XIIᵈ | XIII |
| XIII | XIII | XIV |
| XIV | XIV | XV |
| XV | XV | XVI |
| XVI | XVI | e |
| XVII | XVII | XVII |
| XVIII | XVIII | XVIII |
| XIX | XIX | XIX |
| XX | XX | XX |
| XXᶠ | XXIᵍ | XXI |
| XXI | XXIIʰ | XXII |
| XXII | XXIII | XXIII |
| XXIII | XXIV | XXIV |
| XXIV | XXV | XXV |
| XXV | XXVI | XXVI |
| XXVI | XXVII | XXVII |
| XXVII | XXVIII | XXVIII |
| XXVIII | XXIX | XXIX |
| XXIX | XXX | XXX |
| XXX | XXXI | XXXI |
| XXXI | XXXII | XXXII |
| XXXII | XXXIII | XXXIII |
| XXXIII | XXXIV | XXXIV |
| XXXIV | XXXV | XXXVⁱ |

[a]The second chapter numbered "x"; there is no "xi." [b]English error caught and corrected. [c]The second numbered "xii." [d]Copied the error of the English edition. [e]Chapter xvi was not divided; this makes chapters xvii, xviii, xix, and xx agree in all three editions. [f]The second numbered "xx." [g]English error caught and corrected. [h]From here on numbered one higher than English edition and agreeing with the American. [i]American edition has 35 chapters, correctly numbered; English edition, 36 chapters ending on 34; Canadian, 36 ending on 35.

# Bibliography

The following are some of the more useful sources of information relating to Mark Twain's life and his writing of *Tom Sawyer*. Many additional sources have already been noted in the text; other items can be located in the bibliographies listed below.

Anderson, Frederick, ed. *Mark Twain: The Critical Heritage*. New York: Barnes & Noble, 1971.

Asselineau, Roger. *The Literary Reputation of Mark Twain from 1910 to 1950: A Critical Essay and a Bibliography*. Paris: Marcel Didier, 1954; New York: Gregory Lounz, 1956.

Baldanza, Frank. *Mark Twain: An Introduction and Interpretation*. New York: Barnes & Noble, 1961.

Bee, Maurice, and John Feaster. "Criticism of Mark Twain: A Selected Checklist." *Modern Fiction Studies*, xiv (Spring 1968) 93–139. (Note: This checklist consists of a "General" section and a second headed "Studies of Individual Works." The part specifically directed to *The Adventures of Tom Sawyer* is on pages 122–123.)

Bellamy, Gladys Carmen. *Mark Twain as a Literary Artist*. Norman: University of Oklahoma Press, 1950.

Blair, Walter. *Mark Twain and Huck Finn*. Berkeley: University of California Press, 1960.

————, ed. *Mark Twain's Hannibal, Huck & Tom*. Berkeley: University of California Press, 1969.

Brashear, Minnie M. *Mark Twain: Son of Missouri*. Chapel Hill: University of North Carolina Press, 1934.

Canby, Henry Seidel. *Turn East, Turn West: Mark Twain and Henry James*. Boston: Houghton, Mifflin, 1951.

Clemens, Samuel L. *The Autobiography of Mark Twain: Including Chapters Now Published for the First Time*. As arranged and edited, with an introduction and notes, by Charles Neider. New York: Harper & Brothers, 1959. (Note: Scholars find pros and cons to this version of Mark Twain's *Autobiography*. While Neider has put into better sequence the unorganized material, he also edited others. Some scholars recommend using *Mark Twain's Autobiography*, with an Introduction by Albert Bigelow Paine, 2 vols., New York: Harper & Brothers, 1924.)

————. *Mark Twain in Eruption: Hitherto Unpublished Pages about Men and Events*. Edited with an introduction by Bernard DeVoto. New York: Harper & Brothers, 1940. (Note: More autobiography.)

_____. *Mark Twain's Letters*. Arranged with comment by Albert Bigelow Paine. 2 vols. New York: Harper & Brothers, 1917.

_____. *The Works of Mark Twain*. (Volume 4.) *The Adventures of Tom Sawyer*; *Tom Sawyer Abroad*; *Tom Sawyer, Detective*. Edited by John C. Gerber, Paul Baender, and Terry Firkins. Berkeley: Published for the Iowa Center for Textual Studies by the University of California Press, 1980.

Cox, James M. *Mark Twain: The Fate of Humor*. Princeton, N.J.: Princeton University Press, 1966.

DeVoto, Bernard. *Mark Twain at Work*. Cambridge, Mass.: Harvard University Press, 1942.

_____. *Mark Twain's America*. Boston: Little, Brown, 1932.

Ferguson, DeLancey. *Mark Twain: Man and Legend*. Indianapolis: Bobbs, Merrill, 1943.

French, B.M. *Mark Twain and the Gilded Age*. Dallas: Southern Methodist University Press, 1965.

Hemminghaus, Edgar H. *Mark Twain in Germany*. New York: Columbia University Press, 1939.

Hill, Hamlin L. *Mark Twain and Elisha Bliss*. Columbia: Missouri University Press, 1964.

_____, ed. *Mark Twain's Letters to His Publishers, 1867–1894*. Berkeley: University of California Press, 1967.

Kaplan, Justin. *Mr. Clemens and Mark Twain*. New York: Simon & Schuster, 1966.

Long, E. Hudson. *Mark Twain Handbook*. New York: Hendricks House, 1957.

Lynn, Kenneth S. *Mark Twain and Southwestern Humor*. Boston: Little, Brown, 1960.

McKeithen, Daniel M. *Court Trials in Mark Twain, and Other Essays*. The Hague: Martinus Nijhoff, 1958.

Paine, Albert Bigelow. *Mark Twain, a Biography: The Personal and Literary Life of Samuel Langhorne Clemens*. 3 vols. New York: Harper & Brothers, 1912.

Regan, Robert. *Unpromising Heroes: Mark Twain and His Characters*. Berkeley: University of California Press, 1966.

Rogers, Franklin R. *Mark Twain's Burlesque Patterns as Seen in the Novels and Narratives, 1855–1885*. Dallas: Southern Methodist University Press, 1960.

Scott, Arthur L., ed. *Mark Twain: Selected Criticism*. Dallas: Southern Methodist University Press, 1955.

Smith, Henry Nash. *Mark Twain: The Development of a Writer*. Cambridge, Mass.: Harvard University Press, 1962.

_____, and William M. Gibson, eds. *Mark Twain–Howells Letters: The Correspondence of Samuel L. Clemens and William D. Howells, 1872–1910*. 2 vols. Cambridge, Mass.: Harvard University Press, 1960.

Spengemann, William C. *Mark Twain and the Backwoods Angel: The Matter of Innocence in the Works of Samuel L. Clemens*. Kent, Ohio: Kent University Press, 1966.

Stone, Albert E., Jr. *The Innocent Eye: Childhood in Mark Twain's Imagination*. New Haven, Conn.: Yale University Press, 1961.

Tenny, Thomas Asa. *Mark Twain: A Reference Guide*. Boston: G.K. Hall, 1977. (Note: Supplements to the above volume have appeared annually in *American Literary Realism, 1870–1910*, beginning with Volume x, 1977.)

Weaver, Dwight. *Adventures at Mark Twain Cave*. Jefferson City, Mo.: Discovery Enterprises, 1972 (paper covers).

Webster, Samuel C. *Mark Twain, Business Man*. Boston: Little, Brown, 1946.

Wecter, Dixon, ed. *The Love Letters of Mark Twain*. New York: Harper & Brothers, 1949.

————, ed. *Mark Twain to Mrs. Fairbanks*. San Marino, Calif.: Huntington Library, 1949.

————. *Sam Clemens of Hannibal*. Boston: Houghton, Mifflin, 1952.

Wiggins, Robert A. *Mark Twain: Jackleg Novelist*. Seattle: University of Washington Press, 1964.

# Index

157